Mastering Xamarin.Forms

Build rich, maintainable multiplatform native
mobile apps with Xamarin.Forms

Ed Snider

BIRMINGHAM - MUMBAI

Mastering Xamarin.Forms

First published: January 2016

Production reference: 1250116

Published by Packt Publishing Ltd.
Livery Place
35 Livery Street
Birmingham B3 2PB, UK.

ISBN 978-1-78528-719-0

www.packtpub.com

Credits

Author
Ed Snider

Reviewers
M.I. Isham Mohamed

Vaikesh K P

Commissioning Editor
Dipika Gaonkar

Acquisition Editor
Tushar Gupta

Content Development Editor
Rashmi Suvarna

Technical Editor
Murtaza Tinwala

Copy Editor
Vatsal Surti

Project Coordinator
Judie Jose

Proofreader
Safis Editing

Indexer
Rekha Nair

Production Coordinator
Manu Joseph

Cover Work
Manu Joseph

About the Author

Ed Snider is a senior software engineer, speaker, and Xamarin MVP based in the Washington DC/Northern Virginia area. He has a passion for mobile design and development and regularly speaks about Xamarin and Windows app development at local user groups and community events. Ed is also the founder and organizer of the DC and Northern Virginia Mobile .NET Developers Groups. Ed works at InfernoRed Technology, where his primary role is working with clients and partners to build awesome mobile solutions on the iOS, Android, and Windows platforms. He's been coding for over half of his life, starting out by working part time in high school updating the local newspaper's website and building web apps for small businesses in his hometown. For the first few years of his career as a software developer, Ed worked with Cold Fusion to build dynamic web applications and e-commerce solutions. He started working with the .NET framework when .NET 2.0 came out, building enterprise software with WinForms and ASP.NET, and eventually got into SharePoint solution architecture and development for large federal organizations.

For the past several years, Ed has been focused on building mobile apps with .NET for Windows, iOS, and Android using Xamarin. Ed blogs at www.edsnider.net and can be found on Twitter at www.twitter.com/edsnider.

Acknowledgments

I would like to acknowledge the many people without whom this book would not have been possible.

First and foremost, I want to thank my parents, my wife Kelly, and my two daughters, Camden and Colby, for their loving support, encouragement, and enthusiasm.

Many thanks to Scott Lock, Art Lucia, Josh Blanchard, and all my amazing colleagues at InfernoRed Technology for always inspiring me to learn more and improve myself.

Special thanks to the awesome team at Xamarin, especially Joseph Hill, James Montemagno, Jayme Singleton, Krystin Stutesman, and Spencer Montgomery for their ongoing community support and partnership.

I can't thank the wonderful people at Packt enough for everything they have done to make this book a reality. Thank you Rashmi Suvarna, Tushar Gupta, and Murtaza Tinwala for all your support and patience.

And last but not least, thank you dear reader—I hope you enjoy this book!

About the Reviewers

M.I. Isham Mohamed is a software engineer from Sri Lanka who works for IFS. He was one of the student ambassador for Xamarin. He has given talks on technologies such as Angular JS, C#, .NET, Xamarin, and Microsoft Azure.

> I would like to thank my family. They gave me time to work on this book once I returned from work.

Vaikesh K P is a writer, speaker, daydreamer, and a deep lover of C#. After completing his degree at College of Applied Science, Neruvambram, he started his adventure in the programming career as a software developer for Dimind Innovations. He entered the world of Xamarin through Mono, understanding that the future was going to be smart with mobiles, wearables, and goggles. He moved to Mazsoft Technologies as a .NET/ Xamarin developer, gaining hands-on experience in C#, ASP.Net, XAML, SQLite, MVVM, and MVC, and started creating cool applications for stores. His keen interest in sharing knowledge got him listed as one of the best authors of C# Corner. He believes knowledge is precious and it can be gained only by sharing, which makes him a common participator in tech forums.

www.PacktPub.com

Support files, eBooks, discount offers, and more

For support files and downloads related to your book, please visit www.PacktPub.com.

Did you know that Packt offers eBook versions of every book published, with PDF and ePub files available? You can upgrade to the eBook version at www.PacktPub.com and as a print book customer, you are entitled to a discount on the eBook copy. Get in touch with us at service@packtpub.com for more details.

At www.PacktPub.com, you can also read a collection of free technical articles, sign up for a range of free newsletters, and receive exclusive discounts and offers on Packt books and eBooks.

https://www2.packtpub.com/books/subscription/packtlib

Do you need instant solutions to your IT questions? PacktLib is Packt's online digital book library. Here, you can search, access, and read Packt's entire library of books.

Why subscribe?

- Fully searchable across every book published by Packt
- Copy and paste, print, and bookmark content
- On demand and accessible via a web browser

Free access for Packt account holders

If you have an account with Packt at www.PacktPub.com, you can use this to access PacktLib today and view 9 entirely free books. Simply use your login credentials for immediate access.

Table of Contents

Preface

Xamarin released the Xamarin.Forms toolkit in the summer of 2014, and it
has since become a very popular framework for .NET mobile app developers.
On the surface, Xamarin.Forms is a user interface toolkit focused on abstracting the
platform-specific UI APIs of iOS, Android, and Windows into a single easy-to-use
set of APIs. In addition, Xamarin.Forms also provides the common components
of a Model-View-ViewModel (MVVM) framework, making it extremely easy and
intuitive to bind data to a user interface.

Xamarin.Forms comes with several building blocks that are paramount to a solid
mobile app architecture, such as dependency injection and inversion of control,
messaging, and navigation. However, many apps will quickly outgrow these
"in the box" capabilities and require the use of more advanced and sophisticated
replacements. This book will show you how to leverage the strengths of the Xamarin.
Forms toolkit while complementing it with popular patterns and libraries to achieve
a more robust and sustainable app architecture.

As with any framework or toolkit, there are specific scenarios that it makes more
sense for than others. Xamarin has done a great job of providing guidance and
recommendations on when the use of Xamarin.Forms is appropriate versus when
it might be a better decision to use the core Xamarin platform. Once you have made
the decision to use Xamarin.Forms, this book will help guide you through using
patterns and best practices with your Xamarin.Forms mobile app by walking you
through an end-to-end example.

What this book covers

Chapter 1, Getting Started, will start off by quickly reviewing the basics of the Xamarin.Forms toolkit. We will then walk through building a simple app with Xamarin.Forms, called TripLog. The TripLog app will serve as the foundation that we build upon throughout the rest of the book by applying new techniques and concepts in each subsequent chapter.

Chapter 2, MVVM and Data Binding, will introduce the Model-View-ViewModel (MVVM) pattern and the benefits of using it in a mobile app architecture. We will then walk through updating the TripLog app with ViewModels that provide data for the app's pages through data binding.

Chapter 3, Navigation Service, will explain how navigation works in Xamarin.Forms, some of its shortcomings, and how to overcome them. We will build a custom navigation service for the TripLog app that extends the one provided by Xamarin. Forms to provide a navigation model that occurs solely at the ViewModel level, decoupled from the pages themselves.

Chapter 4, Platform Specific Services and Dependency Injection, will discuss the power of the dependency injection and Inversion of Control (IoC) patterns, specific to multi-platform mobile development. We will discuss how to use a third-party IoC library within the TripLog app, in the place of Xamarin.Forms's default DependencyService. We will then build a couple of services that are dependent on platform-specific APIs and use them within the TripLog app through dependency injection.

Chapter 5, User Interface, will explain how to tap into platform-specific APIs using custom renderers in Xamarin.Forms. We will also discuss the use of value converters to customize the appearance of data at the time of binding.

Chapter 6, API Data Access, will explain how to set up a new API using Microsoft Azure App Services. We will then walk through how to connect the TripLog app to the API to get its data and how to set up caching for offline use.

Chapter 7, Authentication, will explain how to set up authentication on the API created in the previous chapter, and then how to add sign in and authentication to the TripLog app.

Chapter 8, Testing, will discuss the importance of testing in mobile apps. We will walk through how to take advantage of the patterns introduced throughout the book to easily unit test the ViewModels within the TripLog app. We will also use Xamarin's UITest framework to build automated UI tests for the TripLog app that can be run on Xamarin Test Cloud.

Chapter 9, App Analytics, will explain the importance of crash reporting and collecting user data in mobile apps. We will then integrate Xamarin Insights into the TripLog app using the service dependency pattern implemented in *Chapter 4, Platform Specific Services and Dependency Injection*.

Because the focus of this book is on applying patterns and best practices to apps built with Xamarin.Forms and not on the actual specifics of Xamarin.Forms, the chapters will only use a single platform, iOS, for simplicity. However, the architectural concepts in the book will apply to all platforms and any platform-specific code, such as platform services or custom renderers, will be included for iOS, Android, and Windows within the example code that is available for download with the purchase of this book.

What you need for this book

In order to follow along with the code throughout this book, you will need to have Xamarin installed on your machine. The Xamarin installer will take care of installing any SDK prerequisites and will also install Xamarin Studio. Although the examples throughout this book are shown in Xamarin Studio on a Mac, everything shown can also be done in Visual Studio on a Windows machine. If you are using a Windows machine, you will need a Mac running Xamarin on your network to serve as a build host to build and debug iOS apps. For details on setting up a Xamarin build host on a Mac or any other requirement to set up a Xamarin development environment, visit `http://developer.xamarin.com/`.

In *Chapter 6, API Data Access*, you will need a Microsoft Azure account in order to follow along with the examples to create a basic API.

Throughout this book, there are several tools and libraries used which are obtained from NuGet and/or Xamarin's Component Store.

Who this book is for

This book is intended for C# developers who are familiar with the Xamarin platform and Xamarin.Forms toolkit. If you have already started working with Xamarin.Forms and want to take your app to the next level, making it more maintainable, testable, and flexible, then this book is for you.

Conventions

In this book, you will find a number of text styles that distinguish between different kinds of information. Here are some examples of these styles and an explanation of their meaning.

Code words in text, folder names, filenames, file extensions, pathnames, URLs, user input, and Twitter handles are shown as follows: "Add a `TripLogEntry` property to the class and name it `Entry`."

A block of code is set as follows:

```
public MainViewModel : BaseViewModel
{
    public MainViewModel ()
    { ... }
}
```

When we wish to draw your attention to a particular part of a code block, the relevant lines or items are set in bold:

```
public MainViewModel : BaseViewModel
{
    public MainViewModel ()
    {
        Entry = new TripLogEntry ();
    }
}
```

New terms and **important words** are shown in bold. Words that you see on the screen, for example, in menus or dialog boxes, appear in the text like this: "Clicking the **Next** button moves you to the next screen."

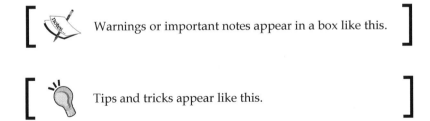

Warnings or important notes appear in a box like this.

Tips and tricks appear like this.

Reader feedback

Feedback from our readers is always welcome. Let us know what you think about this book—what you liked or disliked. Reader feedback is important for us as it helps us develop titles that you will really get the most out of.

To send us general feedback, simply e-mail `feedback@packtpub.com`, and mention the book's title in the subject of your message.

If there is a topic that you have expertise in and you are interested in either writing or contributing to a book, see our author guide at `www.packtpub.com/authors`.

Customer support

Now that you are the proud owner of a Packt book, we have a number of things to help you to get the most from your purchase.

Downloading the example code

You can download the example code files for all Packt books you have purchased from your account at `http://www.packtpub.com`. If you purchased this book elsewhere, you can visit `http://www.packtpub.com/support` and register to have the files e-mailed directly to you.

Downloading the color images of this book

We also provide you with a PDF file that has color images of the screenshots/diagrams used in this book. The color images will help you better understand the changes in the output. You can download this file from `https://www.packtpub.com/sites/default/files/downloads/Mastering_XamarinForms_ColorImages.pdf`.

Errata

Although we have taken every care to ensure the accuracy of our content, mistakes do happen. If you find a mistake in one of our books—maybe a mistake in the text or the code—we would be grateful if you could report this to us. By doing so, you can save other readers from frustration and help us improve subsequent versions of this book. If you find any errata, please report them by visiting `http://www.packtpub.com/submit-errata`, selecting your book, clicking on the **Errata Submission Form** link, and entering the details of your errata. Once your errata are verified, your submission will be accepted and the errata will be uploaded to our website or added to any list of existing errata under the Errata section of that title.

To view the previously submitted errata, go to `https://www.packtpub.com/books/content/support` and enter the name of the book in the search field. The required information will appear under the **Errata** section.

Piracy

Piracy of copyrighted material on the Internet is an ongoing problem across all media. At Packt, we take the protection of our copyright and licenses very seriously. If you come across any illegal copies of our works in any form on the Internet, please provide us with the location address or website name immediately so that we can pursue a remedy.

Please contact us at `copyright@packtpub.com` with a link to the suspected pirated material.

We appreciate your help in protecting our authors and our ability to bring you valuable content.

Questions

If you have a problem with any aspect of this book, you can contact us at `questions@packtpub.com`, and we will do our best to address the problem.

Sources

The iPhone frames used to surround the screenshots in this book were developed by **Andre Revin** (`@andre_revin`). They are available for free on his website at `http://andrerevin.com/iOS7-iPhone-Free-Mockup`.

1
Getting Started

The goal of this book is to focus on how to apply best practices and patterns to mobile apps built with Xamarin.Forms, and not on the actual Xamarin.Forms toolkit and API itself. The best way to achieve this goal is to build an app end-to-end, applying new concepts in each chapter. Therefore, the goal of this first chapter is to simply put together the basic structure of a Xamarin.Forms mobile app codebase, which will serve as a foundation that we can build of off throughout the rest of this book.

In this chapter, we will do the following:

- Introduce and define the features of the app that we will build throughout the rest of the book
- Create a new Xamarin.Forms mobile app with an initial app structure and user interface

Introducing the app idea

Just like the beginning of many new mobile projects, we will start with an idea. We will create a travel app named *TripLog*; and, like the name suggests, it will be an app that will allow its users to log their travel adventures. While the app itself will not be solving any real-world problems, it will have features that will require us to solve real-world architecture and coding problems. The app will take advantage of several core concepts such as list views, maps, location services, and live data from a RESTful API, and we will apply patterns and best practices throughout the rest of this book to implement these concepts.

Defining features

Before we get started, it is important to understand the requirements and features of the TripLog app. We will do this by quickly defining some of the high level things this app will allow its users to do, as follows:

- View existing log entries (online and offline)
- Add new log entries with the following data:
  - Title
  - Location using GPS
  - Date
  - Notes
  - Rating
- Sign into the app

Creating the initial app

To start off the new TripLog mobile app project, we need to create the initial solution architecture. We can also create the core shell of our app's user interface by creating the initial screens based on the basic features we just defined.

Setting up the solution

We will start things off by creating a brand new, blank Xamarin.Forms solution within Xamarin Studio, using the following steps:

1. In Xamarin Studio, click **File | New | Solution**. This will bring up a series of dialog screens that will walk you through creating a new Xamarin.Forms solution. On the first dialog, select **App** on the left, under the **Cross-platform** section, and then select **Xamarin.Forms App** in the middle and click **Next**, as shown in the following screenshot:

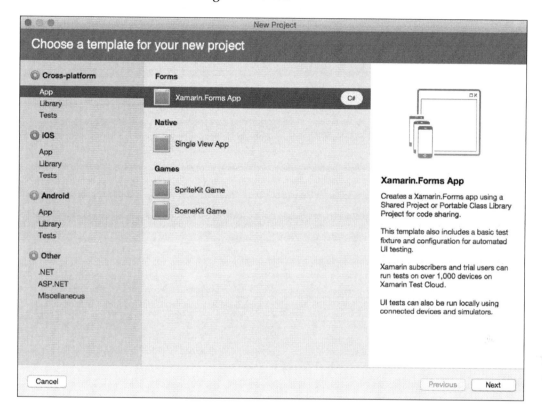

2. On the next dialog screen, enter the name of the app, TripLog, and make sure **Use Portable Class Library** is selected for the **Shared Code** option, as shown in the following screenshot:

3. On the final dialog screen, simply click the **Create** button, as shown in the following screenshot:

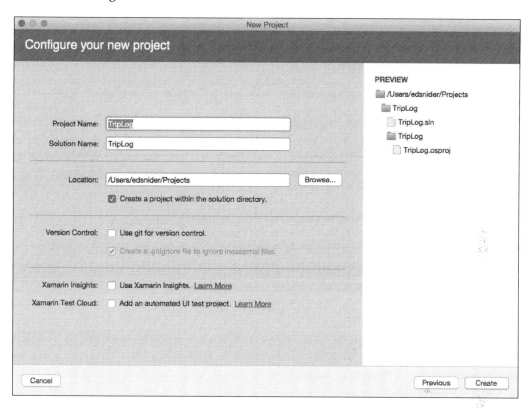

After creating the new Xamarin.Forms solution, you will have several projects created within it, as shown in the following screenshot:

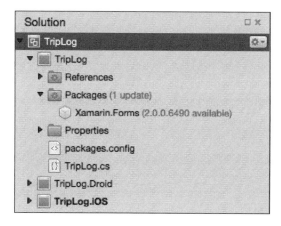

There will be a single portable class library project and two platform-specific projects:

- **TripLog**: This is a portable class library project that will serve as the "core" layer of the solution architecture. This is the layer that will include all of our business logic, data objects, Xamarin.Forms pages, and other non-platform-specific code. The code in this project is common and not specific to a particular platform and therefore can be shared across the platform projects.

- **TripLog.iOS**: This is the iOS platform-specific project containing all of the code and assets required to build and deploy the iOS app from this solution. By default, it will have a reference to the TripLog core project.

- **TripLog.Droid**: This is the Android platform-specific project containing all of the code and assets required to build and deploy the Android app from this solution. By default, it will have a reference to the TripLog core project.

> If you are using Xamarin Studio on a Windows machine, you will only get an Android project when you create a new Xamarin.Forms solution.
>
> In order to include a Windows (WinRT) app in your Xamarin. Forms solution, you will need to use Visual Studio on a Windows machine.
>
> Although the screenshots and samples throughout this book are demonstrated using Xamarin Studio on a Mac, the code and concepts will work in Xamarin Studio and Visual Studio on a Windows machine as well. Refer to the *Preface* for further details on software and hardware requirements that need to be met in order to follow along with the concepts in this book.

You'll notice a file in the core library named **TripLog.cs**, which contains a class named App that inherits from Xamarin.Forms.Application. Initially, the App constructor sets the MainPage property to a new instance of ContentPage that simply displays some default text. The first thing we are going to do in our TripLog app is to build the initial views, or screens, required for our UI, and then update that MainPage property of the App class in **TripLog.cs**.

Updating the Xamarin.Forms packages

If you expand the **Packages** folder within each of the projects in the solution, you will see that Xamarin.Forms is actually a NuGet package that is automatically included when we select the Xamarin.Forms project template. It is possible that the included NuGet packages are out of date and need to be updated, so be sure to update them in each of the projects within the solution, so that you are using the latest version of Xamarin.Forms.

Creating the main page

The main page of the app will serve as the main entry point into the app and will display a list of existing trip log entries. Our trip log entries will be represented by a data model named `TripLogEntry`. Models are a key pillar in the MVVM pattern and data-binding, which we will explore more in *Chapter 2, MVVM and Data Binding*; but in this chapter, we will just create a simple class that will represent the `TripLogEntry` model. Let us now start creating the main page:

1. First, add a new Xamarin.Forms `ContentPage` to the project by right-clicking on the **TripLog** core project, clicking **Add**, and then clicking **New File**. This will bring up the **New File** dialog screen, as shown in the following screenshot:

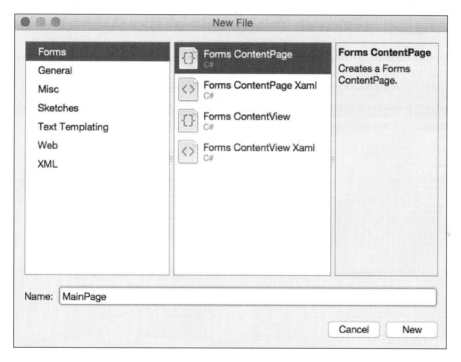

2. On the **New File** dialog screen, select **Forms** in the left pane and then select **Forms ContentPage** in the right pane. Name the new file MainPage and click the **New** button.

3. Next, update the `MainPage` property of the `App` class to a new instance of `Xamarin.Forms.NavigationPage` whose root is a new instance of `TripLog.MainPage` that we just created:

```
public App()
{
    MainPage = new NavigationPage(new TripLog.MainPage());
}
```

4. Create a folder in the **TripLog** core project named **Models**, and create a new empty class file in that folder named `TripLogEntry`.

5. Update the `TripLogEntry` class with the following auto-implemented properties:

```
public class TripLogEntry
{
    public string Title { get; set; }
    public double Latitude { get; set; }
    public double Longitude { get; set; }
    public DateTime Date { get; set; }
    public int Rating { get; set; }
    public string Notes { get; set; }
}
```

6. Now that we have a model to represent our trip log entries, we can use it to display some trips on the main page using a `ListView`. We will use a `DataTemplate` to describe how the model data should be displayed in each of the rows in the `ListView` using the following code:

```
public class MainPage : ContentPage
{
    public MainPage()
    {
        Title = "TripLog";

        var items = new List<TripLogEntry>
        {
            new TripLogEntry
            {
                Title = "Washington Monument",
                Notes = "Amazing!",
                Rating = 3,
                Date = new DateTime(2015, 2, 5),
                Latitude = 38.8895,
```

```
                Longitude = -77.0352
          },
          new TripLogEntry
          {
              Title = "Statue of Liberty",
              Notes = "Inspiring!",
              Rating = 4,
              Date = new DateTime(2015, 4, 13),
              Latitude = 40.6892,
              Longitude = -74.0444
          },
          new TripLogEntry
          {
              Title = "Golden Gate Bridge",
              Notes = "Foggy, but beautiful.",
              Rating = 5,
              Date = new DateTime(2015, 4, 26),
              Latitude = 37.8268,
              Longitude = -122.4798
          }
      };

      var itemTemplate = new DataTemplate (typeof(TextCell));
      itemTemplate.SetBinding (TextCell.TextProperty, "Title");
      itemTemplate.SetBinding (TextCell.DetailProperty, "Notes");

      var entries = new ListView {
          ItemsSource = items,
          ItemTemplate = itemTemplate
      };

      Content = entries;
   }
}
```

Running the app

At this point, we have a single page that is displayed as the app's main page. If we debug the app and run it in a simulator, emulator, or on a physical device, we should see the main page showing the list of the log entries we hard-coded into the view, like in the following screenshot. In *Chapter 2, MVVM and Data Binding,* we will refactor this quite a bit as we implement MVVM and leverage the benefits of data-binding.

Creating the new entry page

The new entry page of the app will give the user a way to add a new log entry by presenting a series of fields to collect the log entry details. There are several ways to build a form to collect data in Xamarin.Forms. You can simply use a `StackLayout` and present a stack of `Label` and `Entry` controls on the screen. You can also use a `TableView` with various types of `ViewCells`. In most cases, a `TableView` will give you a very nice default, platform-specific look-and-feel; however, if your design calls for a more custom look-and-feel, you might be better off leveraging the other layout options available in Xamarin.Forms. For the purposes of this app, we're going to use a `TableView`.

There are some key data points we need to collect when our users log new entries with the app, such as Title, Location, Date, Rating, and Notes. For now, we're going to use a regular `EntryCell` for each of these fields. We will update, customize, and add to these fields later in this book. For example, we will wire the location fields up to a geo-location service that will automatically determine the location, and we will make the date field use an actual platform-specific date picker control; but for now, we're just focused on building the basic app shell.

In order to create the new entry page that contains a `TableView`, perform the following steps:

1. First, add a new Xamarin.Forms `ContentPage` to the project and name it `NewEntryPage`.

2. Update the constructor of the `NewEntryPage` class using the following code to build the **TableView** that will represent the data entry form on the page:

```
public class NewEntryPage : ContentPage
{
    public NewEntryPage ()
    {
        Title = "New Entry";

        // Form fields
        var title = new EntryCell {
            Label = "Title"
        };

        var latitude = new EntryCell {
            Label = "Latitude",
            Keyboard = Keyboard.Numeric
        };

        var longitude = new EntryCell {
            Label = "Longitude",
            Keyboard = Keyboard.Numeric
```

```
        };

        var date = new EntryCell {
            Label = "Date"
        };

        var rating = new EntryCell {
            Label = "Rating",
            Keyboard = Keyboard.Numeric
        };

        var notes = new EntryCell {
            Label = "Notes"
        };

        // Form
        var entryForm = new TableView {
            Intent = TableIntent.Form,
            Root = new TableRoot {
                new TableSection()
                {
                    title,
                    latitude,
                    longitude,
                    date,
                    rating,
                    notes
                }
            }
        };

        Content = entryForm;
    }
}
```

Now that we have created the new entry page, we need to add a way for users to get to this new screen from the main page. We will do this by adding a "New" button to the main page toolbar. In Xamarin.Forms, this is accomplished by adding a ToolbarItem to the base ContentPage ToolbarItems collection and wiring up the ToolbarItem Clicked event to navigate to the new entry page, as shown in the following code:

```
public MainPage ()
{
    var newButton = new ToolbarItem {
        Text = "New"
    };
```

```
newButton.Clicked += (sender, e) => {
    Navigation.PushAsync(new NewEntryPage());
};

ToolbarItems.Add (newButton);

// ...
}
```

In *Chapter 3, Navigation Service*, we will build a custom service to handle navigation between pages, and we will replace the `Clicked` event with a data-bound `ICommand` ViewModel property, but for now, we will use the default Xamarin.Forms navigation mechanism.

Now, when we run the app we will see a **New** button on the toolbar of the main page. Clicking the **New** button should bring us to the **New Entry** page, as shown in the following screenshot:

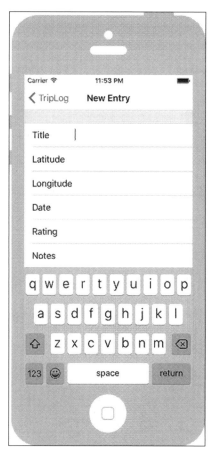

We will need to add a `"Save"` button to the **New Entry** page toolbar, so that we can have a way of saving new items. For now, this button will just be a placeholder in the UI that we will bind an `ICommand` to in *Chapter 2, MVVM and Data Binding*, when we dive into MVVM and data-binding.

The **Save** button will be added to the new entry page toolbar the same way the **New** button was added to the main page toolbar.

In the `NewEntryPage` constructor, simply create a new `ToolbarItem` and add it to the base `ContentPage ToolbarItems` property, as shown in the following code:

```
public NewEntryPage ()
{
    // ...

    var save = new ToolbarItem {
        Text = "Save"
    };

    ToolbarItems.Add (save);

    // ...
}
```

When we run the app again and navigate to the **New Entry** page, we should now see the **Save** button on the toolbar, as shown in the following screenshot:

Creating the entry detail page

When a user taps on one of the log entry items on the main page, we want to take them to a page that displays more details about that particular item, including a map that plots the item's location. Along with additional details and a more in-depth view of the item, a detail page is also a common area where actions on that item might take place, for example, editing the item or sharing the item on social media.

The detail page will take an instance of a `TripLogEntry` model as a constructor parameter, which we will use in the rest of the page to display the entry details to the user.

In order to create the entry detail page, perform the following steps:

1. First, add a new Xamarin.Forms `ContentPage` to the project and name it `DetailPage`.

2. Update the constructor of the `DetailPage` class to take a `TripLogEntry` parameter named entry, as shown in the following code:

    ```
    public class DetailPage : ContentPage
    {
        public DetailPage (TripLogEntry entry)
        {
            // ...
        }
    }
    ```

3. Add the `Xamarin.Forms.Maps` NuGet package to the core project as well as each of the platform-specific projects. This separate NuGet package is required in order to use the Xamarin.Forms `Map` control in the next step.

4. Update the body of the constructor using a `Grid` layout to display the details of the `entry` constructor parameter, as shown in the following code:

    ```
    public DetailPage (TripLogEntry entry)
    {
        Title = "Entry Details";

        var mainLayout = new Grid {
            RowDefinitions = {
                new RowDefinition {
    Height = new GridLength (4, GridUnitType.Star)
                },
                new RowDefinition {
    ```

```
Height = GridLength.Auto
        },
          new RowDefinition {
Height = new GridLength (1, GridUnitType.Star)
        }
      }
    };

    var map = new Map ();

    // Center the map around the log entry's location
    map.MoveToRegion (MapSpan.FromCenterAndRadius (new Position
(entry.Latitude, entry.Longitude), Distance.FromMiles (.5)));

    // Place a pin on the map for the log entry's location
    map.Pins.Add (new Pin {
        Type = PinType.Place,
        Label = entry.Title,
        Position = new Position (entry.Latitude, entry.Longitude)
    });

    var title = new Label {
        HorizontalOptions = LayoutOptions.Center
    };
    title.Text = entry.Title;

    var date = new Label {
        HorizontalOptions = LayoutOptions.Center
    };
    date.Text = entry.Date.ToString ("M");

    var rating = new Label {
        HorizontalOptions = LayoutOptions.Center
    };
    rating.Text = $"{entry.Rating} star rating";

    var notes = new Label {
        HorizontalOptions = LayoutOptions.Center
    };
    notes.Text = entry.Notes;
```

```
var details = new StackLayout {
    Padding = 10,
    Children = {
        title, date, rating, notes
    }
};

var detailsBg = new BoxView {
    BackgroundColor = Color.White,
    Opacity = .8
};

mainLayout.Children.Add (map);
mainLayout.Children.Add (detailsBg, 0, 1);
mainLayout.Children.Add (details, 0, 1);

Grid.SetRowSpan (map, 3);

Content = mainLayout;
}
```

5. Next, we need to wire up the tapped event on the list of items on the MainPage to pass the tapped item over to the DetailPage that we just created, as shown in the following code:

```
entries.ItemTapped += async (sender, e) => {
    var item = (TripLogEntry)e.Item;
    await Navigation.PushAsync (new DetailPage (item));
};
```

6. Finally, we need to initialize the Xamarin.Forms.Maps library in each platform-specific startup class (for example, AppDelegate for iOS and MainActivity for Android) using the following code:

```
global::Xamarin.Forms.Forms.Init ();
Xamarin.FormsMaps.Init ();
LoadApplication (new App ());
```

Now when we run the app and tap on one of the log entries on the main page, we will be navigated to the details page to see more detail about that particular log entry, as shown in the following screenshot:

Summary

In this chapter, we built a simple three-page app with static data, leveraging the most basic concepts of the Xamarin.Forms toolkit. For example, we used the default Xamarin.Forms navigation APIs to move between the three pages, which we will refactor in *Chapter 3, Navigation Service* to use a more flexible, custom navigation service.

Now that we have built the foundation of the app, including the basic UI for each page within the app, we'll begin enhancing the app with better architecture design patterns, live data with offline syncing, nicer looking UI elements, and tests.

In the next chapter, we will introduce the MVVM pattern and data-binding to the app to enforce a separation between the user interface layer and the business and data-access logic.

2
MVVM and Data Binding

In this chapter, we will look at the **Model-View-ViewModel (MVVM)** pattern and the MVVM elements that come with the Xamarin.Forms toolkit, and how we can expand on them to truly take advantage of the power of the pattern. As we dig into these topics, we will apply them to the **TripLog** app that we started building in *Chapter 1, Getting Started*.

In this chapter, we will cover the following:

- Understanding the MVVM pattern and data binding
- MVVM in the Xamarin.Forms toolkit
- Adding the MVVM pattern and data binding to the Xamarin.Forms mobile app created in *Chapter 1, Getting Started*

Understanding the MVVM pattern

At its core, MVVM is a presentation pattern designed to control the separation between user interfaces and the rest of the application. The key elements of the MVVM pattern are as follows:

- **Models**: Models represent the business entities of an application. When responses come back from an API, they are typically deserialized to models.
- **Views**: Views represent the actual pages or screens of an application, along with all of the elements that make them up, including custom controls. Views are very platform-specific and depend heavily on platform APIs to render the application's **user interface (UI)**.

- **ViewModels**: ViewModels control and manipulate the Views by serving as their data context. ViewModels are made up of a series of properties represented by models. These properties are part of what is bound to the Views to provide the data that is displayed to users, or to collect the data that is entered or selected by users. In addition to model-backed properties, ViewModels can also contain commands, which are action-backed properties that bind actual functionality and execution to events that occur in the Views, such as button taps or list item selections.

- **Data binding**: Data binding is the concept of connecting data properties and actions in a ViewModel with the user interface elements in a View. The actual implementation of how data binding happens can vary and in most cases, is provided by a framework, or API. In Windows app development, data binding is provided declaratively in XAML. In traditional (non-Xamarin. Forms) Xamarin app development, data binding is either a manual process or dependent on a framework such as MvvmCross (link to the Mvvmcross site / GitHub page, `https://github.com/MvvmCross/MvvmCross`), a popular framework in the .NET mobile development community. Data binding in Xamarin.Forms follows a very similar approach to Windows app development.

Adding MVVM to the app

The first step of introducing MVVM into an app is to set up the structure by adding folders that will represent the core tenants of the pattern—Models, ViewModels, and Views. Traditionally, the Models and ViewModels live in a core library (usually a portable class library), while the Views live in a platform-specific library. However, thanks to the power of the Xamarin.Forms toolkit and its abstraction of platform-specific UI APIs, the Views in a Xamarin.Forms app can also live in the core library.

> Just because the Views can live in the core library with the ViewModels and Models doesn't mean that separation between the user interface and the app logic isn't important.
>
> In some mobile app architectures, the Models portion of the app might live all alone in its own library so that the models can be shared by other applications or also be used for other purposes.

When implementing a specific structure to support a design pattern, it is helpful to have your application namespaces organized in a similar structure. This is not a requirement but something I find useful. By default, Xamarin Studio does not associate namespaces with directory structures; however, this can be changed in the solution options.

For the TripLog app, I've turned on the naming policy settings to associate namespaces with the directory structure. See *Figure 1* for what these settings should look like in Xamarin Studio:

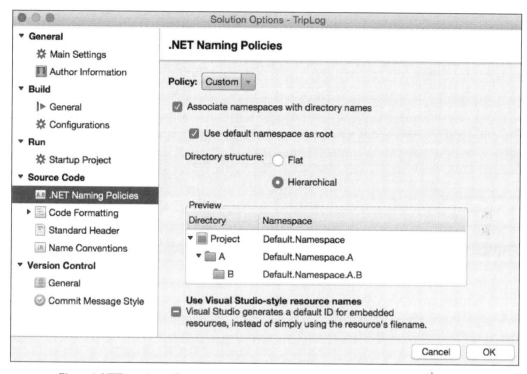

Figure 1 .NET naming policy settings to associate namespaces with the directory structure.

Setting up the app structure

For the TripLog app, we are going to let the Views, ViewModels, and Models all live in the same core portable class library: in our solution, this is the project called TripLog. We already added a Models folder in *Chapter 1, Getting Started*, so we just need to add a ViewModels and Views folder to the project to complete the MVVM structure. In order to set up the app structure, perform the following steps:

1. Add a new folder named ViewModels to the root of the TripLog project.

2. Add a new folder named Views to the root of the TripLog project.

3. Copy the Pages files (MainPage.cs, DetailPage.cs and NewEntryPage.cs) and paste them into the Views folder that we just created.

4. Update the namespace of each Page from TripLog to TripLog.Views.

5. Update the `using` statements on any classes that reference the Pages. Currently, this should only be in the `App` class where `MainPage` is instantiated.

Once the MVVM structure has been added, the folder structure in the solution should look similar to *Figure 2*:

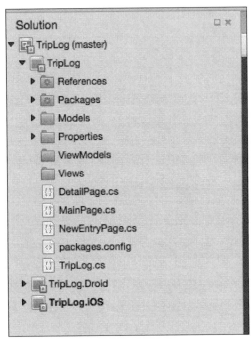

Figure 2 TripLog app structure with MVVM

 In MVVM, the term View is used to describe a screen. Xamarin.Forms uses the term View to describe controls, such as buttons or labels, and uses the term Page to describe a screen. In order to avoid confusion, I will stick with the Xamarin.Forms terminology and refer to screens as Pages, and will only use the term Views to mean screens for the folder where the Pages will live in order to stick with the MVVM pattern.

Adding ViewModels

In most cases, Views (Pages) and ViewModels have a one-to-one relationship; however, it is possible for a View (Page) to contain multiple ViewModels, or for a ViewModel to be used by multiple Views (Pages). For now, we are simply going to have a single ViewModel for each Page. Before we create our ViewModels, we will start by creating a base ViewModel class, which will be an abstract class that contains basic functionality that each of our ViewModels will inherit. Initially, the base ViewModel abstract class will only contain a couple of members and implement INotifyPropertyChanged, but we will add to this class as we continue to build upon the TripLog app throughout the rest of this book.

In order to create a base ViewModel, perform the following steps:

1. Create a new abstract class named BaseViewModel in the ViewModels folder using the following code:

```
public abstract class BaseViewModel
{
    protected BaseViewModel ()
    { }
}
```

2. Update BaseViewModel to implement INotifyPropertyChanged:

```
public abstract class BaseViewModel
        : INotifyPropertyChanged
{
    protected BaseViewModel ()
    { }

    public event PropertyChangedEventHandler PropertyChanged;

    protected virtual void OnPropertyChanged( [CallerMemberName]
string propertyName = null)
    {
        var handler = PropertyChanged;
        if (handler != null)
            handler(this, new PropertyChangedEventArgs (propertyNa
me));
    }
}
```

The implementation of INotifyPropertyChanged is key to the behavior and role of the ViewModels and data binding. It allows a Page to be notified when the properties of its ViewModel have changed.

Now that we have created a base ViewModel, we can start adding the actual ViewModels that will serve as the data context for each of our Pages. We will start by creating a ViewModel for `MainPage`.

Adding MainViewModel

The main purpose of a ViewModel is to separate the business logic, for example data-access, and data-manipulation from the user-interface logic. Right now, our `MainPage` is directly defining the list of data that it is displaying. This data will eventually be dynamically loaded from an API; but for now, we will move this initial static data definition to its ViewModel so that it can be data bound to the user interface.

In order to create the MainPage's ViewModel, perform the following steps:

1. Create a new class file in the `ViewModels` folder and name it `MainViewModel`.

2. Update the `MainViewModel` class to inherit from `BaseViewModel`:

```
public class MainViewModel : BaseViewModel
{
    //...
}
```

3. Add an `ObservableCollection<T>` property to the class called `LogEntries`. This property will be used to bind to the `ItemsSource` property of the `ListView` on `MainPage`:

```
ObservableCollection<TripLogEntry> _logEntries;
public ObservableCollection<TripLogEntry> LogEntries
{
    get { return _logEntries; }
    set {
        _logEntries = value;
        OnPropertyChanged ();
    }
}
```

4. Next, remove the `List<TripLogEntry>` that populates the `ListView` in `MainPage` and repurpose that logic in the `MainViewModel` — we will put it in the constructor for now:

```
public MainViewModel ()
{
    LogEntries = new ObservableCollection<TripLogEntry> ();

    LogEntries.Add (new TripLogEntry {
```

```
            Title = "Washington Monument",
            Notes = "Amazing!",
            Rating = 3,
            Date = new DateTime(2015, 2, 5),
            Latitude = 38.8895,
            Longitude = -77.0352
        });
        LogEntries.Add (new TripLogEntry {
            Title = "Statue of Liberty",
            Notes = "Inspiring!",
            Rating = 4,
            Date = new DateTime(2015, 4, 13),
            Latitude = 40.6892,
            Longitude = -74.0444
        });
        LogEntries.Add (new TripLogEntry {
            Title = "Golden Gate Bridge",
            Notes = "Foggy, but beautiful.",
            Rating = 5,
            Date = new DateTime(2015, 4, 26),
            Latitude = 37.8268,
            Longitude = -122.4798
        });
    }
```

5. Next, set `MainViewModel` as the `BindingContext` for `MainPage` so that it knows where to get the `LogEntries` binding that we created for the `ListView`. Do this by simply setting the `MainPage`'s `BindingContext` property to a new instance of `MainViewModel`. The `BindingContext` property comes from the `Xamarin.Forms.ContentPage` base class:

```
public MainPage ()
{
    BindingContext = new MainViewModel ();
    // ...
}
```

6. Finally, update how the `ListView` on `MainPage` gets its items. Currently, its `ItemsSource` property is being set directly when the `ListView` is created. Remove this setting from the `ListView` object initializer and instead, bind the `MainViewModel` `LogEntries` property to the `ListView` using the `SetBinding` method:

```
var entries = new ListView {
    // ItemsSource = items, <-- Remove this
    ItemTemplate = itemTemplate
};
entries.SetBinding (ListView.ItemsSourceProperty, "LogEntries");
```

Adding DetailViewModel

Next, we will add a ViewModel to serve as the data context for DetailPage, as follows:

1. Create a new class file in the ViewModels folder and name it DetailViewModel.

2. Update the DetailViewModel class to inherit from the BaseViewModel abstract class:

    ```
    public class DetailViewModel : BaseViewModel
    {
        //...
    }
    ```

3. Add a TripLogEntry property to the class and name it Entry. This property will be used to bind to the various labels on DetailPage:

    ```
    TripLogEntry _entry;
    public TripLogEntry Entry
    {
        get { return _entry; }
        set {
            _entry = value;
            OnPropertyChanged ();
        }
    }
    ```

4. Update the DetailViewModel constructor to take a TripLogEntry parameter named entry. Use this constructor property to populate the DetailViewModel public Entry property:

    ```
    public DetailViewModel (TripLogEntry entry)
    {
        Entry = entry;
    }
    ```

5. Next, set DetailViewModel as the BindingContext for DetailPage. Pass in the TripLogEntry property that is being passed to the DetailPage. In *Chapter 3, Navigation Services*, we will refactor how we are passing the entry parameter to DetailPage when we implement a custom navigation service:

    ```
    public DetailPage (TripLogEntry entry)
    {
        BindingContext = new DetailViewModel(entry);
        // ...
    }
    ```

6. Next, update the labels on the `DetailPage` to bind to the properties of the `DetailViewModel` `Entry` property. Do this by removing the code that directly sets the `Text` property of the labels and by using the `SetBinding` method on each label to bind to the appropriate property on the `Entry` model:

```
var title = new Label {
    HorizontalOptions = LayoutOptions.Center
};
// title.Text = entry.Title; <-- Remove this
title.SetBinding (Label.TextProperty, "Entry.Title");

var date = new Label {
    HorizontalOptions = LayoutOptions.Center
};
// date.Text = entry.Date.ToString ("M"); <-- Remove this
date.SetBinding (Label.TextProperty, "Entry.Date",
stringFormat: "{0:M}");

var rating = new Label {
    HorizontalOptions = LayoutOptions.Center
};
// rating.Text = $"{entry.Rating} star rating"; <-- Remove
rating.SetBinding (Label.TextProperty, "Entry.Rating",
stringFormat: "{0} star rating");

var notes = new Label {
    HorizontalOptions = LayoutOptions.Center
};
// notes.Text = entry.Notes; <-- Remove this
notes.SetBinding (Label.TextProperty, "Entry.Notes");
```

7. Finally, update the map to get the values it is plotting from the ViewModel. Because the Xamarin.Forms `Map` control does not have bindable properties, the values have to be set directly to the ViewModel properties. The easiest way to do this is to add a private field to the page that returns the value of the page's `BindingContext` and then use that field to set the values on the `map`:

```
DetailViewModel _vm {
    get { return BindingContext as DetailViewModel; }
}

public DetailPage (TripLogEntry entry)
{
```

```
BindingContext = new DetailViewModel(entry);

// ...

map.MoveToRegion (MapSpan.FromCenterAndRadius (
new Position (_vm.Entry.Latitude, _vm.Entry.Longitude),
    Distance.FromMiles (.5)));

map.Pins.Add (new Pin {
    Type = PinType.Place,
    Label = _vm.Entry.Title,
    Position = new Position (_vm.Entry.Latitude,
_vm.Entry.Longitude)
});

// ...
}
```

Adding NewEntryViewModel

Finally, we need to add the ViewModel for NewEntryPage.

1. Create a new class file in the ViewModels folder and name it
   NewEntryViewModel.

2. Update the NewEntryViewModel class to inherit from BaseViewModel:

```
public class NewEntryViewModel : BaseViewModel
{
    //...
}
```

3. Add properties to the class that will be used to bind to the values entered
   into EntryCell's on NewEntryPage:

```
string _title;
public string Title
{
    get { return _title; }
    set {
        _title = value;
        OnPropertyChanged ();
    }
}

double _latitude;
```

```
public double Latitude
{
    get { return _latitude; }
    set {
        _latitude = value;
        OnPropertyChanged ();
    }
}

double _longitude;
public double Longitude
{
    get { return _longitude; }
    set {
        _longitude = value;
        OnPropertyChanged ();
    }
}

DateTime _date;
public DateTime Date
{
    get { return _date; }
    set {
        _date = value;
        OnPropertyChanged ();
    }
}

int _rating;
public int Rating
{
    get { return _rating; }
    set {
        _rating = value;
        OnPropertyChanged ();
    }
}

string _notes;
public string Notes
{
    get { return _notes; }
    set {
```

```
            _notes = value;
            OnPropertyChanged ();
        }
    }
}
```

4. Update the `NewEntryViewModel` constructor to initialize the `Date` and `Rating` properties:

```
public NewEntryViewModel ()
{
    Date = DateTime.Today;
    Rating = 1;
}
```

5. Add a `Command` property to the class and name it `SaveCommand`. This property will be used to bind to the **Save** `ToolbarItem` on `NewEntryPage`. The Xamarin. Forms `Command` type implements `System.Windows.Input.ICommand` to provide an `Action` to run when the command is executed and a `Func` to determine whether the command can be executed:

```
Command _saveCommand;
public Command SaveCommand
{
    get {
        return _saveCommand ?? (_saveCommand = new Command
(ExecuteSaveCommand, CanSave));
    }
}

void ExecuteSaveCommand()
{
    var newItem = new TripLogEntry {
            Title = this.Title,
            Latitude = this.Latitude,
            Longitude = this.Longitude,
            Date = this.Date,
            Rating = this.Rating,
            Notes = this.Notes
    };
    // TODO: Implement logic to persist Entry in a later chapter.
}

bool CanSave () {
    return !string.IsNullOrWhiteSpace (Title);
}
```

6. In order to keep the `SaveCommand`'s `CanExecute` function up to date, we need to call the `SaveCommand.ChangeCanExecute()` method in any property setters that impact the results of the `CanExecute` function. In our case, this is only the `Title` property:

```
public string Title
{
    get { return _title; }
    set {
        _title = value;
        OnPropertyChanged ();
        SaveCommand.ChangeCanExecute ();
    }
}
```

The `CanExecute` function is not required, but by providing it, you can automatically manipulate the state of the control in the UI that is bound to the `Command` so that it is disabled until all of the required criteria are met, at which point it becomes enabled. *Figure 3* shows how the `CanExecute` function is used to disable the **Save** `ToolbarItem` until **Title** contains a value.

7. Next, set `NewEntryViewModel` as the `BindingContext` for `NewEntryPage`.

```
public NewEntryPage ()
{
    BindingContext = new NewEntryViewModel ();

    // ...
}
```

8. Next, update the `EntryCells` on the `NewEntryPage` to bind to the properties of the `DetailViewModel`. Do this by using the `SetBinding` method on each `EntryCell` to bind to the appropriate ViewModel property:

```
var title = new EntryCell { Label = "Title" };
title.SetBinding (EntryCell.TextProperty, "Title",
BindingMode.TwoWay);

var latitude = new EntryCell {
    Label = "Latitude",
    Keyboard = Keyboard.Numeric
};
```

```
latitude.SetBinding (EntryCell.TextProperty, "Latitude",
BindingMode.TwoWay);

var longitude = new EntryCell {
    Label = "Longitude",
    Keyboard = Keyboard.Numeric
};
longitude.SetBinding (EntryCell.TextProperty, "Longitude",
BindingMode.TwoWay);

var date = new EntryCell { Label = "Date" };
date.SetBinding (EntryCell.TextProperty, "Date",
BindingMode.TwoWay, stringFormat: "{0:d}");

var rating = new EntryCell {
    Label = "Rating",
    Keyboard = Keyboard.Numeric
};
rating.SetBinding (EntryCell.TextProperty, "Rating",
BindingMode.TwoWay);

var notes = new EntryCell { Label = "Notes" };
notes.SetBinding (EntryCell.TextProperty, "Notes",
BindingMode.TwoWay);
```

9. Finally, we need to update the **Save** ToolbarItem on the NewEntryPage to bind to the NewEntryViewModel SaveCommand property:

```
var save = new ToolbarItem { Text = "Save" };
save.SetBinding (ToolbarItem.CommandProperty,
"SaveCommand");
```

Now when we run the app and navigate to the new entry page, we can see the data-binding in action:

Figure 3 CanExecute in action: The Save button is enabled automatically when Title has a value.

Summary

In this chapter, we updated the app that we started creating in *Chapter 1, Getting Started*, by removing data and data-related logic from the pages, off-loading it to a series of ViewModels, and then binding the Pages to those ViewModels. In the next chapter, we are going to expand on Xamarin.Forms navigation service, so that we can also move navigation code from the views to the ViewModels.

3
Navigation Service

The overarching goal of this book is to show how you can build a solid architecture based on design patterns and best practices; the objective of this chapter is to take our TripLog app one step closer to achieving that goal. By introducing MVVM into our TripLog app in *Chapter 2, MVVM and DataBinding*, we set up the app with a very clear pattern to separate the user interface from the rest of the logic in the app. Each subsequent chapter, starting with this one, further advances this concept of separation.

In *Chapter 2, MVVM and DataBinding*, we moved a large portion of the app logic into ViewModels; however, navigation is still being initiated from the pages (or views). In this chapter, we're going to move navigation into ViewModels as well.

Here is a quick look at what we'll cover in this chapter:

- Understanding the basics of the Xamarin.Forms navigation API
- Thinking about navigation in MVVM
- Creating a navigation service
- Updating the TripLog app to use the navigation service

The Xamarin.Forms navigation API

Along with abstracting common user interface elements into a cross-platform API, Xamarin.Forms also abstracts navigation for iOS, Android, and Windows into a single, easy to use navigation service. Each mobile platform does navigation slightly different and has a slightly different navigation API; however, at their core, they all accomplish similar tasks and in most cases use a stack structure — last in, first out.

The Xamarin.Forms navigation API uses stack-like terminology, closely resembling the navigation APIs of iOS. The Xamarin.Forms navigation API is exposed through the `Xamarin.Forms.INavigation` interface, which is implemented via the `Navigation` property that can be called from any `Xamarin.Forms.VisualElement` object, but typically, `Xamarin.Forms.Page`. The `Xamarin.Forms.NavigationPage` also implements the `INavigation` interface and exposes public methods to perform common navigation tasks.

The Xamarin.Forms navigation API supports two types of navigation: standard and modal. Standard navigation is the typical navigation pattern where the user clicks or taps through a series of pages and is able to use either device/operating-system provided (back buttons on Android and Windows Phone) functionality or app provided (navigation bar on iOS and action bar on Android) elements to navigate back through the stack. Modal navigation is similar to the modal dialog concept in web apps where a new page is layered on top of the calling page, preventing interaction with the calling page until the user performs a specific action to close the modal page. On smaller form factor devices, modal pages typically take up the entire screen, whereas on larger form factors, such as tablets, modal pages may only take up a sub-set of the screen, more like a dialog. The `INavigation` interface exposes two separate read-only properties to view the standard and modal navigation stacks: `NavigationStack` and `ModalStack`.

The `Xamarin.Forms.INavigation` interface provides several methods to asynchronously push and pop pages onto the navigation and modal stacks:

- `PushAsync(Page page)` and `PushAsync(Page page, bool animated)` to navigate to a new page.
- `PopAsync()` and `PopAsync(bool animated)` to navigate back to the previous page, if there is one.
- `PushModalAsync(Page page)` and `PushModalAsync(Page page, bool animated)` to modally display a page.
- `PopModalAsync()` and `PopModalAsync(bool animated)` to dismiss the current modally displayed page.

In addition to these methods, there are also a few methods that help you manipulate the navigation stack, since it is exposed as a read-only property:

- `InsertPageBefore(Page page, Page before)` to insert a page before a specific page that is already in the navigation stack
- `RemovePage(Page page)` to remove a specific page in the navigation stack
- `PopToRootAsync()` and `PopToRootAsync(bool animated)` to navigate back to the first page and remove all others in the navigation stack

We've already used `PushAsync` a few times in the TripLog app to allow the user to move from page to page. In the next couple of sections of this chapter, we'll create a custom navigation service that extends the Xamarin.Forms navigation API, use it to move those instances of `PushAsync` from the pages into the ViewModels, and expose them through commands that will be data-bound to the page.

Navigation and MVVM

One of the key purposes of the MVVM pattern is to isolate an app's presentation layer from its other layers; in doing so, an app's business logic is also isolated. One of the thoughts behind this isolation is to have a user interface that is only concerned with displaying data and that is completely independent of how that data is stored, acquired, manipulated, or shared with the rest of the app. As explained in *Chapter 2, MVVM and DataBinding*, this is typically accomplished through databinding. In MVVM, the actions that a user takes on a page are bound to commands on that page's backing ViewModel. It is very common for actions to result in a transition to another page—either by directly linking to it or by automatically navigating to a previous page after performing a task, such as saving data. Because of this, it makes sense to rethink how we do navigation in an app that leverages the MVVM pattern so that it can be controlled by ViewModels and not by the pages.

Most common third-party MVVM frameworks and toolkits subscribe to this theory and often even provide a navigation service that is designed for ViewModel consumption.

There are a couple of approaches to consider when performing navigation within ViewModels. One approach is page-centric and the other is ViewModel-centric. A page-centric approach involves navigating to another page by a direct reference to that page. A ViewModel-centric approach involves navigating to another page by reference to that page's ViewModel.

The page-centric approach can be accomplished in Xamarin.Forms by simply passing the current `Xamarin.Forms.INavigation` instance into a ViewModel's constructor. From there, the ViewModel can use the Xamarin.Forms default navigation mechanism to navigate to other pages. The benefits of this approach are that it separates the navigation functionality from the page layer, and it's fairly quick to implement. However, the downside is that is puts a strong dependency on direct page references into ViewModels. I typically prefer to use the ViewModel-centric approach and keep ViewModels loosely coupled and agnostic of the actual page implementations.

ViewModel-centric navigation

As previously discussed, the ViewModel-centric approach alleviates a ViewModel of having any dependencies on the specific implementation of individual pages. In a default Xamarin.Forms solution, this might not appear to be such a big deal, but imagine if pages were self-contained in their own library—the library containing ViewModels probably wouldn't have a reference to that library. This is typical of a traditional Xamarin-based cross-platform solution architecture, and a good practice to follow.

Because ViewModel doesn't navigate directly to a page, it will navigate to a page via the page's ViewModel. This means that when implementing this approach, there is a need to build a relationship, or mapping, between pages and their ViewModels. As with most things in software, this can be done in a couple of ways. One way is to include a dictionary or key-value type property in the navigation service that maintains a one-to-one mapping of pages and ViewModels using their `Type`. This could also be done external of the navigation service to provide additional abstraction. Another approach that is employed by the **MVVM Light** (`http://mvvmlight.codeplex.com/`) toolkit's navigation service is to map the `Type` of ViewModel with a `String` key that represents the actual pages.

In the next section, we'll create a ViewModel-centric navigation service that includes ViewModel and page `Type` mapping.

Creating a navigation service

In a typical cross-platform mobile app architecture, one would have to implement a platform-specific navigation service for each platform the app supports. In our case, Xamarin.Forms has already done this, so we're simply going to implement a single navigation service that extends the Xamarin.Forms navigation abstraction so we can perform ViewModel to ViewModel navigation.

The first thing we need to do is define an interface for our navigation service that will define its methods. We are starting with an interface so the service can be added to ViewModels via constructor injection, which we'll dive into in *Chapter 4, Platform Specific Services and Dependency Injection*. We are also starting with an interface so we can easily provide alternative implementations of the service without changing ViewModels that depend on it. A common scenario for this is creating a mock of the service that gets used when unit testing ViewModels.

In order to create the navigation service, perform the following steps:

1. Create a new `Services` folder in the core library and within it create a new interface named `INavService`:

```
public interface INavService
{
    bool CanGoBack { get; }

    Task GoBack ();

    Task NavigateTo<TVM> ()
        where TVM : BaseViewModel;

    Task NavigateTo<TVM, TParameter> (TParameter parameter)
        where TVM : BaseViewModel;

    Task RemoveLastView ();

    Task ClearBackStack ();

    Task NavigateToUri (Uri uri);

    event PropertyChangedEventHandler CanGoBackChanged;
}
```

This interface defines fairly standard navigation behavior – the ability to navigate to ViewModels, the ability to navigate back, the ability to clear the navigation stack, as well as the ability to navigate to a regular URI. The `NavigateTo` method defines a generic type, and restricts its use to objects of the `BaseViewModel` base class, which we created in the previous chapter. There is also an overloaded `NavigateTo` method that enables a strongly typed parameter to be passed along with the navigation.

Before we create the actual implementation of the `INavService` interface, we need to make a couple updates to our `BaseViewModel`:

1. Update the `BaseViewModel` to include an abstract `Init` method:

```
public abstract Task Init ();
```

This `Init` method provides ViewModels with a way of initializing without using the constructor, which is useful when a ViewModel needs to be refreshed.

2. Next, add a second `BaseViewModel` abstract base class with a generic-type that will be used to pass strongly typed parameters to the `Init` method:

```
public abstract class BaseViewModel<TParameter>
    : BaseViewModel
{
    protected BaseViewModel () : base ()
    { }

    public override async Task Init()
    {
        await Init (default(TParameter));
    }

    public abstract Task Init (TParameter parameter);
}
```

3. Next, update `MainViewModel` and `NewEntryViewModel` to override the `Init` method; for now, the `NewEntryViewModel Init` will just be a blank implementation.

    The `Init` method in `MainViewModel` will be responsible for loading the log entries. We will move the log entry list population logic out of the constructor and into a new `async` method called `LoadEntries`, which will be called from the `Init` override:

```
public MainViewModel () : base ()
{
    LogEntries = new ObservableCollection<TripLogEntry> ();
}

public override async Task Init ()
{
    await LoadEntries ();
}

async Task LoadEntries()
{
    LogEntries.Clear ();

    await Task.Factory.StartNew (() => {
        LogEntries.Add (new TripLogEntry {
            Title = "Washington Monument",
            Notes = "Amazing!",
            Rating = 3,
```

```
                Date = new DateTime(2015, 2, 5),
                Latitude = 38.8895,
                Longitude = -77.0352
            });
            LogEntries.Add (new TripLogEntry {
                Title = "Statue of Liberty",
                Notes = "Inspiring!",
                Rating = 4,
                Date = new DateTime(2015, 4, 13),
                Latitude = 40.6892,
                Longitude = -74.0444
            });
            LogEntries.Add (new TripLogEntry {
                Title = "Golden Gate Bridge",
                Notes = "Foggy, but beautiful.",
                Rating = 5,
                Date = new DateTime(2015, 4, 26),
                Latitude = 37.8268,
                Longitude = -122.4798
            });
        });
}
```

4. Next, update `DetailViewModel` to inherit from
    `BaseViewModel<TripLogEntry>` and override the `Init` method and
    set the `Entry` property with the value of its `TripLogEntry` parameter:

```
public class DetailViewModel : BaseViewModel<TripLogEntry>
{
    // ...

    public DetailViewModel ()
    {

    }

    public override async Task Init (TripLogEntry logEntry)
    {
        Entry = logEntry;
    }
}
```

Notice that because we are now setting the `Entry` property within the `Init`
method, we can remove the `TripLogEntry` parameter from the constructor.

5. We also need to remove the `TripLogEntry` parameter from the `DetailPage` constructor as it will now be all handled between the navigation service and the ViewModel's `Init` method:

```
public class DetailPage : ContentPage
{
    public DetailPage () // <- Remove parameter
    {
        // ...
    }

    // ...
}
```

Now that `BaseViewModel` has been updated, we can create our navigation service that implements `INavService`.

6. Create a new class within the `Services` folder of the core library. Name the new class `XamarinFormsNavService` and make it implement `INavService`:

```
public class XamarinFormsNavService : INavService
{
}
```

7. Update the `XamarinFormsNavService` to include a public `INavigation` property named `XamarinFormsNav`. This `XamarinFormsNav` property provides a reference to the current `Xamarin.Forms.INavigation` instance and will need to be set when the navigation service is first initialized, which we'll see later in this section when we update the TripLog app:

```
public class XamarinFormsNavService : INavService
{
    public INavigation XamarinFormsNav { get; set; }

    // INavService implementation goes here.
}
```

As discussed in the previous section, we will implement the navigation service with a page-to-ViewModel mapping. We will do this with an `IDictionary<Type, Type>` property and a method to register the mappings.

8. Update the `XamarinFormsNavService` with an `IDictionary<Type, Type>` readonly property and add a public method to populate it named `RegisterViewMapping`:

```
readonly IDictionary<Type, Type> _map = new Dictionary<Type, Type>();
```

```
public void RegisterViewMapping (Type viewModel, Type view)
{
    _map.Add (viewModel, view);
}
```

9. Next, implement the INavService methods. Most of the INavService methods will leverage the XamarinFormNav property to make calls to the Xamarin.Forms navigation API in order to perform navigation and alter the navigation stack:

```
public bool CanGoBack {
    get {
        return XamarinFormsNav.NavigationStack != null
            && XamarinFormsNav.NavigationStack.Count > 0;
    }
}

public async Task GoBack ()
{
    if (CanGoBack) {
        await XamarinFormsNav.PopAsync(true);
    }

    OnCanGoBackChanged ();
}

public async Task NavigateTo<TVM> ()
    where TVM : BaseViewModel
{
    await NavigateToView (typeof(TVM));

    if (XamarinFormsNav.NavigationStack
        .Last().BindingContext is BaseViewModel)
        await ((BaseViewModel)(XamarinFormsNav
        .NavigationStack.Last ().BindingContext)).Init ();
}

public async Task NavigateTo<TVM, TParameter> (TParameter
parameter)
    where TVM : BaseViewModel
{
    await NavigateToView (typeof(TVM));

    if (XamarinFormsNav.NavigationStack
    .Last().BindingContext is BaseViewModel<TParameter>)
```

```
        await ((BaseViewModel<TParameter>)(XamarinFormsNav
          .NavigationStack.Last ().BindingContext))
          .Init (parameter);
}

async Task NavigateToView(Type viewModelType)
{
    Type viewType;

    if (!_map.TryGetValue (viewModelType, out viewType))
        throw new ArgumentException ("No view found in View
Mapping for " + viewModelType.FullName + ".");

    var constructor = viewType.GetTypeInfo ()
.DeclaredConstructors
.FirstOrDefault(dc => dc.GetParameters ().Count() <= 0);
    var view = constructor.Invoke (null) as Page;

    await XamarinFormsNav.PushAsync (view, true);
}

public async Task RemoveLastView ()
{
    if (XamarinFormsNav.NavigationStack.Any())
    {
            var lastView = XamarinFormsNav.NavigationStack
[XamarinFormsNav.NavigationStack.Count - 2];
        XamarinFormsNav.RemovePage(lastView);
    }
}

public async Task ClearBackStack ()
{
    if (XamarinFormsNav.NavigationStack.Count <= 1)
        return;

for (var i = 0; i < XamarinFormsNav.NavigationStack.Count - 1;
i++)
     XamarinFormsNav.RemovePage
        (XamarinFormsNav.NavigationStack [i]);
}

public async Task NavigateToUri (Uri uri)
{
    if (uri == null)
```

```
        throw new ArgumentException("Invalid URI");

    Device.OpenUri(uri);
}


public event PropertyChangedEventHandler CanGoBackChanged;

void OnCanGoBackChanged()
{
    var handler = CanGoBackChanged;
    if (handler != null)
        handler(this, new
            PropertyChangedEventArgs("CanGoBack"));
}
```

10. Finally, the navigation service class needs to be marked as a dependency so that it can be resolved by the Xamarin.Forms DependencyService. This is accomplished by adding an assembly attribute to the class, before the namespace block, as shown in the following code block:

```
[assembly: Dependency(typeof(XamarinFormsNavService))]
namespace TripLog.Services
{
    public class XamarinFormsNavService : INavService
    { ... }
}
```

In *Chapter 4, Platform Specific Services and Dependency Injection*, we will remove this as we replace the Xamarin.Forms DependencyService with a third-party IoC and dependency injection library.

Updating the TripLog app

With the navigation service complete, we can now update the rest of the TripLog app to leverage it. To start with, we will update the constructor in the main App class to create a new instance of the navigation service and register the app's page-to-ViewModel mappings:

```
public App ()
{
    // The root page of your application
    var mainPage = new NavigationPage(new MainPage());

    var navService = DependencyService.Get<INavService>() as
XamarinFormsNavService;
```

```
    navService.XamarinFormsNav = mainPage.Navigation;

    navService.RegisterViewMapping (typeof(MainViewModel),
typeof(MainPage));
    navService.RegisterViewMapping (typeof(DetailViewModel),
typeof(DetailPage));
    navService.RegisterViewMapping (typeof(NewEntryViewModel),
typeof(NewEntryPage));

    MainPage = mainPage;
}
```

Updating BaseViewModel

Since most ViewModels in the TripLog app will need to use the navigation service, it makes sense to include it in the `BaseViewModel` class:

```
public abstract class BaseViewModel : INotifyPropertyChanged
{
    protected INavService NavService { get; private set; }

    protected BaseViewModel (INavService navService)
    {
        NavService = navService;
    }

    // ...
}
```

Each of the ViewModels that inherit from `BaseViewModel` will need to be updated to include an `INavService` parameter in their constructors that is passed to the `BaseViewModel` class. The `BaseViewModel<TParameter>` base class needs to be updated to include an `INavService` constructor parameter as well.

In addition, each ViewModel initialization needs to be updated to pass in an `INavService`, which can be retrieved from the Xamarin.Forms `DependencyService`:

1. Update the `MainViewModel` instantiation in the `MainPage` constructor:

    ```
    public MainPage ()
    {
        BindingContext = new MainViewModel (
            DependencyService.Get<INavService> ());

        // ...
    }
    ```

2. Update the `DetailViewModel` instantiation in the `DetailPage` constructor:

```
public DetailPage (TripLogEntry entry)
{
    BindingContext = new DetailViewModel (
        DependencyService.Get<INavService> ());

    // ...
}
```

3. Update the `NewEntryViewModel` instantiation in the `NewEntryPage` constructor:

```
public NewEntryPage ()
{
    BindingContext = new NewEntryViewModel (
        DependencyService.Get<INavService> ());

    // ...
}
```

Updating MainViewModel

In order to move navigation functionality from `MainPage` to `MainViewModel`, we need to add two new `Command` properties — one for creating a new log entry and one for viewing the details of an existing log entry:

```
Command<TripLogEntry> _viewCommand;
public Command<TripLogEntry> ViewCommand {
    get { return _viewCommand
?? (_viewCommand = new Command<TripLogEntry> (async (entry) => await
ExecuteViewCommand(entry))); }
}

Command _newCommand;
public Command NewCommand {
    get { return _newCommand
?? (_newCommand = new Command (async () => await ExecuteNewCommand
()))); }
}

async Task ExecuteViewCommand(TripLogEntry entry)
{
    await NavService.NavigateTo<DetailViewModel, TripLogEntry>
(entry);
}
```

```
async Task ExecuteNewCommand()
{
    await NavService.NavigateTo<NewEntryViewModel> ();
}
```

With the `Commands` in place on `MainViewModel`, we can now update `MainPage` to use these commands instead of using the Xamarin.Forms navigation service directly from the page:

1. Create a private `MainViewModel` property named `_vm` in the `MainPage` class that simply provides access to the page's `BindingContext`, but casted as a `MainViewModel` type:

   ```
   public class MainPage : ContentPage
   {
       MainViewModel _vm {
           get { return BindingContext as MainViewModel; }
       }

       // ...
   }
   ```

2. Update the `ItemTapped` event on the `entries` `ListView` to call the `ViewCommand`:

   ```
   entries.ItemTapped += async (sender, e) => {
       var item = (TripLogEntry)e.Item;
       _vm.ViewCommand.Execute(item);
   };
   ```

3. Replace the `Clicked` event on the `newButton` `ToolbarItem` with a `Binding` to the `NewCommand`:

   ```
   newButton.SetBinding (ToolbarItem.CommandProperty, "NewCommand");
   ```

Initializing MainViewModel

The `XamarinFormsNavService` custom navigation service we created handles initializing ViewModels automatically when they are navigated to by calling the `Init` method in `BaseViewModel`. However, because the main page is launched by default and not via navigation, we need to manually call the `Init` method on the page's ViewModel when the page first appears.

Update the `MainPage` by overriding its `OnAppearing` method to call its ViewModel's `Init` method:

```
protected override async void OnAppearing ()
{
    base.OnAppearing ();

    // Initialize MainViewModel
    if (_vm != null)
        await _vm.Init();
}
```

Updating NewEntryViewModel

In *Chapter 2, MVVM and DataBinding,* we already added `SaveCommand` to `NewEntryViewModel`; however, once the `SaveCommand` executed, nothing occurred. Once `SaveCommand` performs its logic to save the new log entry, it should navigate the user back to the previous page. We can accomplish this by updating `SaveCommand`'s execute `Action` to call the `GoBack` method in the navigation service that we created in the last section:

```
async Task ExecuteSaveCommand ()
{
    var newItem = new TripLogEntry {
            Title = this.Title,
            Latitude = this.Latitude,
            Longitude = this.Longitude,
            Date = this.Date,
            Rating = this.Rating,
            Notes = this.Notes
    };

    // TODO: Implement logic to persist Entry in a later chapter.

    await NavService.GoBack ();
}
```

Notice that because the `ExecuteSaveCommand` method now calls an asynchronous method, it needs to use `async` and `await` and its return type needs to be updated from `void` to `Task`.

Updating DetailPage

Finally, we need to update how the map on `DetailPage` is being bound to the data in the `DetailViewModel`. Because the ViewModel is being initialized via the navigation service now, it happens after the page is constructed, and therefore the map doesn't have the data it needs. Normally, this would not be a problem thanks to data binding, but since the map control does not allow for data binding we need to handle its data differently. The best way for the page to check when its ViewModel has data for its map control is to handle the ViewModel's `PropertyChanged` event. If the ViewModel's `Entry` property changes, the map control should be updated accordingly, as shown in the following steps:

1. First, update the map to a private class property named _map:

```
public class DetailPage : ContentPage
{
    // ...

    readonly Map _map;

    public DetailPage ()
    {
        // ...

        // var map = new Map ();
        _map = new Map ();

        // ...

        mainLayout.Children.Add (_map);
        mainLayout.Children.Add (detailsBg, 0, 1);
        mainLayout.Children.Add (details, 0, 1);

        Grid.SetRowSpan (_map, 3);

        Content = mainLayout;
    }
}
```

2. Next, move the two statements that center and the plot points on the map control out of the constructor and into a separate private method in the `DetailPage` class:

```
void UpdateMap ()
{
    if (_vm.Entry == null)
        return;

    // Center the map around the log entry's location
    _map.MoveToRegion (MapSpan.FromCenterAndRadius (
        new Position (_vm.Entry.Latitude,
            _vm.Entry.Longitude),
        Distance.FromMiles (.5)
    ));

    // Place a pin on the map for the log entry's location
    _map.Pins.Add (new Pin {
        Type = PinType.Place,
        Label = _vm.Entry.Title,
        Position = new Position (_vm.Entry.Latitude,
            _vm.Entry.Longitude)
    });
}
```

3. Finally, handle the ViewModel's `PropertyChanged` event to update the map when the ViewModel's `Entry` property is changed:

```
public DetailPage ()
{
    BindingContextChanged += (sender, args) =>
    {
        if (_vm == null) return;

        _vm.PropertyChanged += (s, e) => {
            if (e.PropertyName == "Entry")
                UpdateMap ();
        };
    };

    // ...
}
```

Summary

In this chapter, we created a service that extends the default Xamarin.Forms navigation API to enable ViewModel-centric navigation, enforcing a better separation between the presentation layer and the business logic in ViewModels.

In *Chapter 4, Platform Specific Services and Dependency Injection*, we're going to create some additional services that abstract platform-specific APIs and replace the Xamarin.Forms DependencyService with a more flexible IoC and dependency injection alternative.

4
Platform Specific Services and Dependency Injection

This chapter will not attempt to teach everything there is to know about **Inversion of Control (IoC)** and dependency injection, as there are numerous resources available that strictly focus on these topics alone. Instead, this chapter will focus on how these patterns apply to mobile development and, more specifically, how to implement them in a Xamarin.Forms mobile app.

Here is a quick look at what we'll cover in this chapter:

- The need for dependency injection in multi-platform mobile app development
- Implementing IoC and dependency injection using a third-party library in place of the Xamarin.Forms DependencyService
- Creating, injecting, and using platform-specific services
- Updating our TripLog app to use platform-specific services through IoC and dependency injection

Inversion of control and dependency injection in mobile apps

In software development, IoC and dependency injection solve many problems. In the world of mobile development, specifically multi-platform mobile development, they provide a great pattern to handle platform and device-specific code. One of the most important aspects to multi-platform mobile development is the idea of sharing code. Not only does development become easier and quicker when code can be shared across apps and platforms, but also maintenance, management, feature parity, and so on. However, there are always parts of an application's codebase that simply cannot be shared due to its strict tie in with the platform's APIs. In most cases, an app's user interface represents a large portion of this non-sharable code. It is because of this that the MVVM pattern makes so much sense in multi-platform mobile development—it forces the separation of user interface code (Views) into individual platform-specific libraries, making it easy to then compartmentalize the rest of the code (ViewModels and Models) into a single, sharable library.

But what if the code in the shared ViewModels needs to do something like access the device's physical geo-location, or leverage the device's camera to take a photo? Because the ViewModels exist in a single platform-agnostic library, they can't call the platform specific APIs. This is where dependency injection saves the day.

The Xamarin.Forms DependencyService versus third-party alternatives

In addition to providing the core building blocks for the MVVM pattern, Xamarin. Forms also includes a very basic service to handle dependency registration and resolution, the DependencyService. We actually used this service in the preceding chapter to register and resolve our custom navigation service. Like many of the services and components built into the Xamarin.Forms toolkit, the DependencyService is designed to help get users up and running quickly by providing an easy-to-use basic implementation. It is in no way the only way of handling dependencies in a Xamarin.Forms mobile app and, in most complex apps, you will quickly outgrow the capabilities of the Xamarin.Forms DependencyService. For example, the Xamarin. Forms DependencyService doesn't provide a way of doing constructor injection. There are several third-party alternatives to the DependencyService that allow much greater flexibility, such as Autofac, TinyIoC, Ninject, and Unity, among others. Each of these libraries are open sourced and, in most cases, community maintained. They all implement the patterns in slightly different ways and offer different key benefits depending on the architecture of your app.

In the next couple of sections, we will build two new platform-specific services and use the Ninject library to register and use them in our TripLog app. We will also update the navigation service from *Chapter 3, Navigation Service,* to be registered in Ninject, instead of the Xamarin.Forms DependencyService.

Creating and using platform-specific services

We already created a service in the preceding chapter to handle navigation. That custom navigation service specification was provided by an interface, INavService, and there is a property of that interface type in the BaseViewModel so that a concrete implementation of the service can be provided to the ViewModels as needed.

The benefit of using an interface to define platform-specific services is that it can be used in an agnostic way in the ViewModels and the concrete implementations can be provided via dependency injection. Those concrete implementations can be actual services, or even mocked services for unit testing the ViewModels, as we'll see in *Chapter 8, Testing.*

In addition to navigation, there are a couple of other platform-specific services our TripLog app could use to enrich its data and experience. In this section, we will create a location service that allows us to get specific geo-coordinates from the device. The actual platform-specific implementation of the location service is fairly trivial and there are tons of resources on how to do this in various ways. We will create a basic implementation without going too deep so that we can keep the focus on how we leverage it as a dependency in a Xamarin.Forms architecture.

Similar to the approach taken for the navigation service, we will first start out by creating an interface for the location service and then create the actual platform-specific implementations.

Creating a location service

The first step to allowing our app to take advantage of the device's geo-location capabilities is to provide an interface in the core library that can be used by the ViewModels in a device and platform agnostic manner. When getting geo-location back from a device, each platform could potentially provide coordinates in a platform-specific data structure. However, each structure will ultimately provide two double values representing the coordinate's latitude and longitude values. There are a couple of ways to ensure the results are returned in a platform-agnostic manner, which we need since we are working in a portable class library.

One way is to pass the values back via a callback method. Another approach, which we will employ, is to use a custom object, which we will define in our `Models` namespace, as shown in the following steps:

1. Create a new class named `GeoCoords` in the `Models` folder of the core TripLog project.

2. Add two `double` properties to the `GeoCoords` class named `Latitude` and `Longitude`:

```
public class GeoCoords
{
    public double Latitude { get; set; }
    public double Longitude { get; set; }
}
```

3. Create a new interface named `ILocationService` in the `Services` folder of the core TripLog project. The interface should have one `async` method, which returns a `GeoCoords` object:

```
public interface ILocationService
{
    Task<GeoCoords> GetGeoCoordinatesAsync();
}
```

Using the location service on the new entry page

Now that we have an interface that defines our location service, we can use it in the core project of our TripLog app. The main place we need to capture location in the app is on the new entry page, so coordinates can be attached to log entries when they are added. Because we want to keep our app logic separated from the user interface, we will use the location service in the new entry page's ViewModel, and not on the `Page` itself.

In order to use the `ILocationService` in the `NewEntryViewModel`, perform the following steps:

1. First, add a `readonly` property to the `NewEntryViewModel` to hold an instance of the location service:

```
public class NewEntryViewModel : BaseViewModel
{
    readonly ILocationService _locService;
    // ...
}
```

2. Next, update the `NewEntryViewModel` constructor to take an `ILocationService` instance and set its readonly `ILocationService` property:

```
public NewEntryViewModel (INavService navService, ILocationService
locService)
    : base (navService)
{
    _locService = locService;

    Date = DateTime.Today;
    Rating = 1;
}
```

3. Finally, update the `NewEntryViewModel Init` method to use the location service to set the `Latitude` and `Longitude` on the `Entry` property:

```
public override async Task Init ()
{
    var coords = await
        _locService.GetGeoCoordinatesAsync ();

    Latitude = coords.Latitude;
    Longitude = coords.Longitude;
}
```

As you can see, we can completely work with our location service in the ViewModel even though we haven't actually written the platform-specific implementation. Although, if we run the app, we will get a runtime error, because the implementation won't actually exist, but it's useful to be able to work with the service through abstraction to fully build out and test the ViewModel.

Adding the location service implementation

Now that we have created an interface for our location service and updated the ViewModel to use it, we need to create the concrete platform-specific implementations. For the purposes of this chapter, we will only create the iOS and Android implementations; however, the companion code for this book contains the Windows implementation as well.

In order to tap into the platform's geo-location capabilities, we can leverage a Xamarin Component named Xamarin.Mobile. The Xamarin.Mobile Component provides an easy API to use device-specific utilities such as geo-location, media, and contacts, as shown in the following steps:

1. First, add the Xamarin.Mobile Component to each of the platform projects (that is, `TripLog.iOS` and `TripLog.Droid`) by right-clicking on the `Components` folder.

2. Next, create a new folder in the `TripLog.iOS` project named `Services`, and within it, create a new class named `LocationService` that implements the `ILocationService` interface we created earlier in the chapter:

```
public class LocationService : ILocationService
{
    public async Task<GeoCoords> GetGeoCoordinatesAsync ()
    {
        var locator = new Geolocator {
            DesiredAccuracy = 30
        };

        var position = await
            locator.GetPositionAsync (30000);

        var result = new GeoCoords {
            Latitude = position.Latitude,
            Longitude = position.Longitude
        };

        return result;
    }
}
```

3. Finally, create a new folder in the `TripLog.Droid` project named `Services`, and within it, create a new class named `LocationService` that implements the `ILocationService` interface we created earlier in the chapter. When using the Xamarin.Mobile Component to create a location service, the iOS and Android implementations are almost identical. The only major difference between the two implementations is that Android requires the `Geolocator` to be instantiated with the current Android Activity. In Xamarin.Forms, this can be accessed via the `Context` property of the static `Forms` class:

```
public class LocationService : ILocationService
{
    public async Task<GeoCoords> GetGeoCoordinatesAsync ()
    {
```

```
            var locator = new Geolocator (Forms.Context) {
                DesiredAccuracy = 30
        };

            var position = await
                locator.GetPositionAsync (30000);

            var result = new GeoCoords {
                Latitude = position.Latitude,
                Longitude = position.Longitude
            };

        return result;
        }
    }
```

On iOS 8.0 and higher, you must enable location requests in the application's `Info.plist`.

On Android, you must require `ACCESS_COARSE_LOCATION` and `ACCESS_FINE_LOCATION` in the application's manifest.

Now that we have created a platform-dependent service, it is time to register it into an IoC container so that we can use it throughout the rest of the code. In the next section, we will use Ninject to create registrations between our location service interface and the actual platform-specific implementations. We will also update the custom navigation service that we created in *Chapter 3, Navigation Service*, to use Ninject in place of the default Xamarin.Forms DependencyService.

Registering dependencies

As mentioned earlier, each IoC and dependency injection library implements the patterns slightly differently. In this section, we will use Ninject to start adding dependency injection capabilities to our TripLog app. Ninject allows you to create **Modules**, which are responsible for adding services to the IoC container. The modules are then added to a **Kernel** that is used to resolve the services by other areas of the app.

You can create a single Ninject Module or many, depending on how your app is structured and how you want to organize your services. For the TripLog app, we will have a Ninject Module in each platform project that is responsible for registering that platform's specific service implementations. We will also create a Ninject Module in the core library that will be responsible for registering dependencies that live in the core library, such as ViewModels and data access services, which we will add later in *Chapter 6, API Data Access*, when we start working with live data.

Registering the platform-service implementations

We will start by creating Ninject Modules in each of the platform projects that will be responsible for registering their respective platform's specific service implementations, as shown in the following steps:

1. Add the Portable.Ninject NuGet package to each of the platform-specific projects—`TripLog.iOS` and `TripLog.Droid`.

2. Next, create a new folder in the `TripLog.iOS` project named `Modules`, and within it, create a new class named `TripLogPlatformModule` that inherits from `Ninject.Modules.NinjectModule`:

    ```
    public class TripLogPlatformModule : NinjectModule
    {
        // ...
    }
    ```

3. Override the `Load` method of the `NinjectModule` class and use the Ninject `Bind` method to register the iOS-specific implementation of `ILocationService` as a singleton:

    ```
    public class TripLogPlatformModule : NinjectModule
    {
        public override void Load ()
        {
            Bind<ILocationService> ()
            .To<LocationService> ()
            .InSingletonScope ();
        }
    }
    ```

4. Next, create a folder in the `TripLog.Droid` project named `Modules`, and within it, create a new class named `TripLogPlatformModule` that inherits from `Ninject.Modules.NinjectModule`:

    ```
    public class TripLogPlatformModule : NinjectModule
    {
        // ...
    }
    ```

5. Finally, override the `Load` method of the `NinjectModule` class and use the Ninject `Bind` method to register the Android-specific implementation of `ILocationService` as a singleton:

    ```
    public class TripLogPlatformModule : NinjectModule
    {
    ```

```
    public override void Load ()
    {
        Bind<ILocationService> ()
        .To<LocationService> ()
        .InSingletonScope ();
    }
}
```

Registering the ViewModels

We can also use our IoC container to hold our ViewModels. It is a slightly different model than the one used to register concrete implementations of our service interfaces—instead of mapping them to an interface, we are simply registering them to themselves.

Because our ViewModels are in our core library, we will create another Ninject Module in the core library, a core module, that will handle registering them, as shown in the following steps:

1. Add the Portable.Ninject NuGet package to the core project.

2. Create a new folder in the core project named Modules, and within it, create a new class named TripLogCoreModule that inherits from Ninject.Modules.NinjectModule:

```
public class TripLogCoreModule : NinjectModule
{
    // ...
}
```

3. Override the Load method of the NinjectModule class and use the Ninject Bind method to register each of the ViewModels:

```
public class TripLogCoreModule : NinjectModule
{
    public override void Load ()
    {
        // ViewModels
        Bind<MainViewModel> ().ToSelf ();
        Bind<DetailViewModel> ().ToSelf ();
        Bind<NewEntryViewModel> ().ToSelf ();
    }
}
```

Registering the navigation service

In the previous chapter, we created a custom navigation service and used the Xamarin.Forms DependencyService to register and resolve it. Now that we have introduced Ninject, we can swap Xamarin.Forms DependencyService out and use a Ninject Module to register the navigation service instead so that it can be resolved and used just like our platform-specific services.

1. The only change we need to make to the navigation service itself is to remove the `assembly` attribute that was added above the class's namespace:

```
// Remove assembly attribute
// [assembly: Dependency(typeof(XamarinFormsNavService))]
```

   We originally instantiated the navigation service and registered view mappings all within the core `App` class. We can now move all of that logic into a new Ninject Module. However, in order for us to instantiate our navigation service, we require an instance of `Xamarin.Forms.INavigation`, so we will have to set this new Module up to take that in as a constructor parameter, and then its overridden `Load` method will handle creating the service, creating the view mappings, and then registering the service into the IoC.

2. Create a new class in the core project `Modules` folder named `TripLogNavModule` that inherits from `NinjectModule`:

```
public class TripLogNavModule : NinjectModule
{
    // ...
}
```

3. Update the constructor of the `TripLogNavModule` to take in a `Xamarin.Forms.INavigation` parameter:

```
public class TripLogNavModule : NinjectModule
{
    readonly INavigation _xfNav;

    public TripLogNavModule (INavigation xamarinFormsNavigation)
    {
        _xfNav = xamarinFormsNavigation;
    }
}
```

4. Override the `Load` method of the `NinjectModule` class to instantiate a new `XamarinFormsNavService` object:

```
public override void Load ()
{
```

```
        var navService = new XamarinFormsNavService ();
        navService.XamarinFormsNav = _xfNav;
}
```

5. Remove the ViewModel-to-View mappings from the `App` class and put them into the `TripLogNavModule Load` override method:

```
public override void Load ()
{
    var navService = new XamarinFormsNavService ();
    navService.XamarinFormsNav = _xfNav;

    // Register view mappings
    navService.RegisterViewMapping (
      typeof(MainViewModel),
      typeof(MainPage));

    navService.RegisterViewMapping (
        typeof(DetailViewModel),
        typeof(DetailPage));

    navService.RegisterViewMapping (
        typeof(NewEntryViewModel),
        typeof(NewEntryPage));
}
```

6. Finally, update the `TripLogNavModule Load` override method to use the Ninject `Bind` method to register the `XamarinFormsNavService` object as a singleton:

```
public override void Load ()
{
    var navService = new XamarinFormsNavService ();
    navService.XamarinFormsNav = _xfNav;

    // Register view mappings
    navService.RegisterViewMapping (
        typeof(MainViewModel),
        typeof(MainPage));

    navService.RegisterViewMapping (
        typeof(DetailViewModel),
        typeof(DetailPage));

    navService.RegisterViewMapping (
        typeof(NewEntryViewModel),
```

```
        typeof(NewEntryPage));

    Bind<INavService> ()
        .ToMethod (x => navService)
        .InSingletonScope ();
}
```

 Platform-specific services are good candidates for singleton objects. ViewModels can be singletons, but typically should not be.

Updating the TripLog app

Now that our platform services, navigation service, and ViewModels have all been registered with the IoC, we need to add the Ninject Modules that we created to the Ninject Kernel. We will do this in our main `Xamarin.Forms.Application` class, App.

In order to get our platform modules into the App class, which is in our core library, we will simply update the App constructor to take in `INinjectModule` parameters. Then, each platform-specific project will be responsible to pass in its respective Ninject module when it loads the App at startup.

1. Update the App constructor to take in `INinjectModule` parameters:

    ```
    public App (params INinjectModule[] platformModules)
    {
        // ...
    }
    ```

2. Next, add a public `IKernel` property named `Kernel` to the App class:

    ```
    public class App : Application
    {
        public IKernel Kernel { get; set; }

        // ...
    }
    ```

3. Next, update the body of the App constructor. In the previous section, we moved the bulk of the existing App constructor logic into the navigation Ninject Module. Now the App constructor should only be responsible for creating the main page and initializing the Ninject Kernel with the various modules we have created:

    ```
    public App (params INinjectModule[] platformModules)
    {
    ```

```
var mainPage = new NavigationPage (new MainPage ());

// Register core services
Kernel = new StandardKernel (
    new TripLogCoreModule (),
    new TripLogNavModule(mainPage.Navigation));

// Register platform specific services
Kernel.Load (platformModules);

// Get the MainViewModel from the IoC
mainPage.BindingContext = Kernel.Get<MainViewModel> ();

MainPage = mainPage;
}
```

Notice how we get an instance of the `MainViewModel` from the IoC container and use it to set the ViewModel of the `MainPage`. In the next section, we'll update the navigation service to do this same thing each time we navigate to the other pages in the app.

4. Finally, we need to update the `App` instantiation in the `AppDelegate` class of our iOS project to pass in a new instance of `TripLog.iOS.Modules.TripLogPlatformModule`:

   ```
   LoadApplication (new App (new TripLogPlatformModule()));
   ```

5. The same thing needs to be done in the `MainActivity` class of the Android project.

Updating the navigation service to handle ViewModel creation and dependency injection

Currently in the TripLog app, each page is responsible for creating its own ViewModel instance. However, because we provide a ViewModel's dependencies through its constructor, we would have to manually resolve each dependency within the `Page` class and pass them into the ViewModel instantiation. Not only is this going to be messy code, it is also difficult to maintain and doesn't promote loose coupling. Because we have registered our ViewModels in our IoC, we can completely remove the ViewModel instantiations from our `Pages` and set our navigation service up to handle resolving the ViewModels from the IoC, automatically supplying their dependencies through constructor injection.

1. First, remove the code from the constructor of each Page that sets its `BindingContext` property to a new ViewModel instance.

2. Next, update the `NavigateToView` private method in the `XamarinFormsNavService` to handle setting the ViewModels of the Pages automatically as they are navigated to. After the Page (view) is created using the `Invoke` method, simply get a new instance of the specified ViewModel and set it to the `BindingContext` of the Page:

```
async Task NavigateToView(Type viewModelType)
{
    // ...

    var view = constructor.Invoke (null) as Page;

    var vm = ((App)Application.Current).Kernel.GetService
(viewModelType);
    view.BindingContext = vm;

    await XamarinFormsNav.PushAsync (view, true);
}
```

Summary

In this chapter, we explored the benefits of the dependency injection and IoC patterns in mobile development, and how they help solve the problem of working with platform-specific APIs from shared code. We also made some significant improvements to our Xamarin.Forms TripLog app by adding a new platform-specific service and introducing the Ninject dependency injection library resulting in a codebase that is more flexible and easier to test.

In the next chapter, we're going to shift our focus back to the View layer of our app and we will enhance the user experience with some customizations and leverage some of the platform capabilities we are now surfacing through our ViewModels.

5
User Interface

Here is a quick look at what we'll cover in this chapter:

- How to leverage platform-specific APIs to extend the default behavior of Xamarin.Forms controls with **Custom Renderers**
- How to manipulate the visual appearance of bound data with **Value Converters**

Custom Renderers

One of the paramount features of the Xamarin.Forms toolkit is the layer of abstraction it provides over user interface implementation. With a single API, Xamarin.Forms allows you to use native user interface controls and functionality. For example, the `Entry` class at runtime will display a `UITextField` view on iOS, an `EditText` widget on Android, and a `TextBox` control on Windows. The toolkit does this by using a concept called **Renderers**. The renderers correspond with the visual elements — controls, pages, and layouts — within the API. So, for example, there is an `EntryRenderer` that is responsible for rendering instances of the `Entry` class down to the platform-specific versions of that control.

The beauty of this renderer concept is that you can subclass the various renderer classes to override how a specific element is translated at runtime. So, for example, if you wanted all textboxes in your app (that is, every time you display an `Entry` element) to be completely borderless, you could simply write a new `EntryRenderer` sub-class for each platform that removes the border on the platform-specific element. However, you typically won't want to completely override the default controls of the toolkit. The more common solution is to create a custom control by sub-classing a Xamarin.Forms element and then writing the renderer specifically for that custom class. So then, instead of removing the border from all uses of `Entry`, you would instead use a custom `Entry` class, for example `NoBorderEntry`, that, when rendered, will be borderless.

The concept of Custom Renderers is a very powerful and handy utility when building rich apps using the Xamarin.Forms toolkit. Using the default controls and behaviors of the toolkit will certainly render a native experience, but they can limit you in more complex scenarios. Custom Renderers will ensure that you can exceed these limits when needed to deliver the exact experience you want.

Creating a TableView DatePicker

In our TripLog app, we are using a `TableView` with `EntryCells` to present a form to the user to add a new log entry. Currently, the date field in the form is using a regular `EntryCell` that presents an editable text field with the default keyboard. Obviously, this is not an ideal user experience, and it also causes a nightmare when it comes to data validity. Ideally, when the user taps into this date field, they should be presented with a standard, platform-specific date picker.

The Xamarin.Forms API provides the `DatePicker` control; however, it is based on a `View`, not a `ViewCell`. The only way to use the `DatePicker` control in a `TableView` would be to wrap it in a `ViewCell`, as follows:

```
var datePickerCell = new ViewCell {
    View = new DatePicker()
};
```

While this approach will work, it is somewhat limited. It is simply a control embedded in a `ViewCell`; it does not have the same look and feel as the rest of the cells in the `TableView`. In order to get a similar look and feel to the `EntryCells` used in the `TableView`, you would have to add a label and also mess with the margins, spacing, and sizing to get it to look just right. Another minor downside to this approach is that, in order to capture both date and time, you will need to include two separate cells—one that includes `DatePicker`, and one that includes `TimePicker`. The iOS `UIDatePicker` actually provides a mode that lets the user pick both the date and time in the same picker. Android does not have this same capability; but if we're going to make a Custom Renderer, we can at least take advantage of the dual mode on iOS.

So, in order to overcome these limitations and deliver the best experience possible, we can create a Custom Renderer that extends the `EntryCellRenderer` to display an `EntryCell` that behaves like the standard `DatePicker` control.

Because we don't want to render all `EntryCells` in our application with date picker
functionality, the first thing we need to do is a create a custom `EntryCell` control
that the Custom Renderer will be affiliated with. We can create this in a `Controls`
folder within the core library of our TripLog app, as follows:

1. First, create a new folder in the core project named `Controls` and, within
   it, create a new class named `DatePickerEntryCell` that inherits from
   `EntryCell`:

```
public class DatePickerEntryCell : EntryCell
{
}
```

2. Next, add a `DateTime BindableProperty` so that this custom control can be
   data bound just like any other control:

```
public class DatePickerEntryCell : EntryCell
{
    public static readonly BindableProperty DateProperty =
        BindableProperty
            .Create<DatePickerEntryCell, DateTime>(p =>
                p.Date,
                DateTime.Now,
                propertyChanged: new BindableProperty
                    .BindingPropertyChangedDelegate<DateTime>(
                        DatePropertyChanged));

    public DateTime Date
    {
        get { return (DateTime)GetValue(DateProperty); }
        set { SetValue(DateProperty, value); }
    }

    public new event EventHandler Completed;

    static void DatePropertyChanged(BindableObject bindable,
        DateTime oldValue,
        DateTime newValue)
    {
        var @this = (DatePickerEntryCell)bindable;

        if (@this.Completed != null)
            @this.Completed(bindable, new EventArgs());
    }
}
```

Notice how the `Completed` EventHandler is used in conjunction with the `DateProperty` PropertyChanged event so we can respond to the `Completed` events on our `DatePickerEntryCell` just like we can with a standard `EntryCell`.

Next, we need to create a custom `EntryCellRenderer` that will provide the platform-specific functionality for the `DatePickerEntryCell`, as follows:

1. Create a new folder in the TripLog.iOS project named `Renderers` and, within it, create a new class named `DatePickerEntryCellRenderer` that inherits `EntryCellRenderer`, as follows:

```
public class DatePickerEntryCellRenderer
    : EntryCellRenderer
{
    // ...
}
```

2. Next, override the `EntryCellRenderer` `GetCell` method to override the default `EntryCell` behavior for iOS by setting `InputView` of `UITextField` to a `UIDatePicker` instance:

```
public class DatePickerEntryCellRenderer
    : EntryCellRenderer
{
    public override UITableViewCell GetCell (Cell item,
        UITableViewCell reusableCell, UITableView tv)
    {
        var cell = base.GetCell (item, reusableCell, tv);

        var datepickerCell = (DatePickerEntryCell)item;

        UITextField textField = null;

        if (cell != null)
            textField = (UITextField)cell.ContentView
                            .Subviews [0];

        // Default datepicker display attributes
        var mode = UIDatePickerMode.Date;
        var displayFormat = "d";
        var date = NSDate.Now;
        var isLocalTime = false;

        // Update datepicker based on Cell's properties
        if (datepickerCell != null) {
            // Kind must be Universal or Local to cast to
```

```
        // NSDate
        if (datepickerCell.Date.Kind == DateTimeKind.
Unspecified) {
            var local = new DateTime (datepickerCell.Date.Ticks,
DateTimeKind.Local);
            date = (NSDate)local;
        }
        else
            date = (NSDate)datepickerCell.Date;

        isLocalTime = datepickerCell.Date.Kind == DateTimeKind.
Local || datepickerCell.Date.Kind == DateTimeKind.Unspecified;
    }

    // Create iOS datepicker
    var datepicker = new UIDatePicker {
        Mode = mode,
        BackgroundColor = UIColor.White,
        Date = date,
        TimeZone = isLocalTime ? NSTimeZone.LocalTimeZone
                               : new NSTimeZone("UTC")
    };

    // Create a toolbar with a done button that will
    // close the datepicker and set the selected value
    var done = new UIBarButtonItem("Done",
UIBarButtonItemStyle.Done, (s, e) => {
        var pickedDate = (DateTime)datepicker.Date;

        if (isLocalTime)
            pickedDate = pickedDate.ToLocalTime();

        // Update the Date property on the Cell
        if (datepickerCell != null)
            datepickerCell.Date = pickedDate;

        // Update the value of the UITextField within the
        // Cell
        if (textField != null)
        {
            textField.Text = pickedDate.
ToString(displayFormat);
            textField.ResignFirstResponder();
```

```
            }
        });

        var toolbar = new UIToolbar {
            BarStyle = UIBarStyle.Default,
            Translucent = false
        };

        toolbar.SizeToFit ();
        toolbar.SetItems (new[] { done }, true);

        // Set the input view, toolbar and initial value for
        // the Cell's UITextField
        if (textField != null) {
            textField.InputView = datepicker;
            textField.InputAccessoryView = toolbar;

            if (datepickerCell != null)
                textField.Text = datepickerCell.Date.ToString
(displayFormat);
        }

        return cell;
    }
}
```

3. Next, in order to register the Custom Renderer, simply add an `ExportRenderer` assembly attribute to the class above the namespace declaration. This attribute is required by Xamarin.Forms in order for the Custom Renderer to take action on the control at runtime:

```
[assembly: ExportRenderer(typeof(DatePickerEntryCell), typeof(Date
PickerEntryCellRenderer))]
```

4. Finally, we need to update our `NewEntryPage` to use our new custom `DatePickerEntryCell`. Simply update the current date object from `EntryCell` to `DatePickerEntryCell` and update the binding to use `DateProperty`:

```
var date = new DatePickerEntryCell {
    Label = "Date"
};
date.SetBinding (DatePickerEntryCell.DateProperty,
    "Date",
    BindingMode.TwoWay);
```

Now, if we run the TripLog app by navigating to the new entry page and tapping into the date field, we will see a native date picker as shown in the next image. As we pick different values in the picker, the `DateProperty` binding we created will automatically update the ViewModel as well.

 The Android version of this Custom Renderer is available in the companion source code for this book.

Value Converters

Value Converters form an important concept in data-binding because they allow you to customize the appearance of a data property at the time of binding. If you have done any WPF or Windows app development, you are probably familiar with how Value Converters work. Xamarin.Forms provides an almost identical Value Converter interface as part of its API.

One of the biggest benefits to a Value Converter is that it prevents you from having to add a bunch of getter properties to your data model to adjust how things are displayed. For example, imagine you had a status property on your model and you wanted to change the font color of the status when it is displayed based on its value. You could add a getter property to your model that returns a color based on the current value of the status property. This approach works, but it clutters the model and also potentially leaks platform-specific and user interface logic into the model, which should typically remain very lean and agnostic. The more appropriate approach is to create a Value Converter that allows you to bind directly to the status property, but display it differently based on the value.

Another common way that Value Converters are helpful in Xamarin.Forms is to toggle visibility of elements based on a Boolean property. Luckily, the Xamarin.Forms API made the `VisualElement IsVisible` property into a Boolean instead of an enumeration; so showing things based on Boolean properties is fairly straight forward. However, if you want to hide something when a data bound property is true, you will need a Value Converter to convert the true value to a false value when it is bound to `IsVisibleProperty` of an element.

In the next section, we will create a reverse visibility converter that we will use to hide controls on the screen until the ViewModel has finished loading. We'll also create a converter that converts our integer rating property to stars for a more appealing visual effect.

Creating a reverse visibility Value Converter

There are often cases where your user interface must wait for data to be loaded; in the meantime, the user might see what appears to be a broken or incomplete page. In these situations, it is best to let the user know what is happening by showing some sort of progress indicator and hiding the rest of the user interface, such as labels, until the data is ready.

Right now, our TripLog app is only using local data, so we do not really see any negative visual effects while the ViewModel data is loaded. We will connect our app to a live API in the next chapter, but until then, we can simulate a waiting period by simply adding a three second delay to our `MainViewModel LoadEntries` method before the `LogEntries` collection is populated:

```
async Task LoadEntries()
{
    LogEntries.Clear ();

    // TODO: Remove this in Chapter 6
    await Task.Delay (3000);

    // ...
}
```

Now, if we run the app, while the list of entries is being loaded, we just see an awkwardly half loaded page as shown in the next image. The empty `ListView` is not only unappealing, there is also no visual indicator to explain to the user that their data is on its way.

We can improve this by hiding the ListView until the data is loaded and by showing an ActivityIndicator while it's loading.

In order to know if our ViewModel is loading data, we can create a boolean property called IsBusy that we only set to true while we are actually loading data or doing some sort of lengthy processing. Since we will need to do similar things in other ViewModels, it makes the most sense to include this IsBusy property on the BaseViewModel:

1. Add a public bool property named IsBusy to the BaseViewModel class, as follows:

```
bool _isBusy;
public bool IsBusy
{
    get { return _isBusy; }
    set
    {
        _isBusy = value;
        OnPropertyChanged();
        OnIsBusyChanged();
    }
}
protected virtual void OnIsBusyChanged()
{
}
```

2. Next, we need to update the LoadEntries method in MainViewModel to toggle the IsBusy value while it's loading data:

```
async Task LoadEntries()
{
    if (IsBusy)
        return;

    IsBusy = true;

    LogEntries.Clear ();

    // TODO: Remove this in Chapter 6
    await Task.Delay (3000);
```

```
LogEntries.Add (new TripLogEntry {
    Title = "Washington Monument",
    Notes = "Amazing!",
    Rating = 3,
    Date = new DateTime(2015, 2, 5),
    Latitude = 38.8895,
    Longitude = -77.0352
});
LogEntries.Add (new TripLogEntry {
    Title = "Statue of Liberty",
    Notes = "Inspiring!",
    Rating = 4,
    Date = new DateTime(2015, 4, 13),
    Latitude = 40.6892,
    Longitude = -74.0444
});
LogEntries.Add (new TripLogEntry {
    Title = "Golden Gate Bridge",
    Notes = "Foggy, but beautiful.",
    Rating = 5,
    Date = new DateTime(2015, 4, 26),
    Latitude = 37.8268,
    Longitude = -122.4798
});

IsBusy = false;
}
```

Now that our ViewModel indicates when it is busy, we need to update the UI on
MainPage to hide the ListView when data is loading and to show a loading indicator
instead. We will do this by data binding the IsBusy property in two places. In order
to hide the ListView when IsBusy is true, we will need to create a reverse Boolean
Value Converter.

1. Create a new folder in the core project named Converters, and, within
    it, create a new file named ReverseBooleanConverter that implements
    Xamarin.Forms.IValueConverter:

```
public class ReverseBooleanConverter : IValueConverter
{
}
```

2. Next, implement the `Convert` and `ConvertBack` methods of `IValueConverter`. The goal of this converter is to return the opposite of a given Boolean value; so, when something is false, the converter will return true:

```
public class ReverseBooleanConverter : IValueConverter
{
    public object Convert (object value, Type targetType,
object parameter, System.Globalization.CultureInfo culture)
    {
        if (!(value is Boolean))
            return value;

        return !((Boolean)value);
    }

    public object ConvertBack (object value,
Type targetType, object parameter,
System.Globalization.CultureInfo culture)
    {
        if (!(value is Boolean))
            return value;

        return !((Boolean)value);
    }
}
```

3. Now, we can bind the `IsBusy` property to the `ListView` on the `MainPage` using this converter, so it is only visible (`IsVisible` is true) when `IsBusy` is false:

```
public MainPage ()
{
    // ...

    var entries = new ListView {
        ItemTemplate = itemTemplate
    };

    entries.SetBinding (ListView.ItemsSourceProperty,
        "LogEntries");
```

```
entries.SetBinding (ListView.IsVisibleProperty,
"IsBusy",
converter: new ReverseBooleanConverter ());

// ...
}
```

4. Finally, we need to add a loading indicator to the MainPage and only show it when IsBusy is true. We'll do this by adding an ActivityIndicator and a label to a StackLayout, and displaying it in the center of the screen. Also, because we now have two elements to show on the screen, we need to update how we're setting Content:

```
public MainPage ()
{
    // ...

    var loading = new StackLayout {
        Orientation = StackOrientation.Vertical,
        HorizontalOptions = LayoutOptions.Center,
        VerticalOptions = LayoutOptions.Center,
        Children = {
            new ActivityIndicator { IsRunning = true },
            new Label { Text = "Loading Entries..." }
        }
    };

    loading.SetBinding (StackLayout.IsVisibleProperty,
"IsBusy");

    var mainLayout = new Grid {
        Children = { entries, loading }
    };

    Content = mainLayout;
}
```

Now, when we launch the app, we will see a nice loading indicator while the data loads instead of a blank list view, as shown in the following screenshot:

Creating an integer to image Value Converter

In this section we're going to continue to improve the user experience with the use of another Value Converter. Currently, the DetailPage binds to the Rating property and simply displays the integer value in a formatted string, which is a rather boring way to display that data, as shown in the following screenshot:

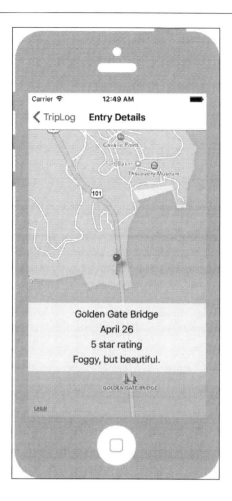

This rating data would look much nicer and stand out to the user much quicker if it were an image of stars instead of plain text. In order to translate a number value to an image, we will need to create a new Value Converter.

1. Create a new file in the core library Converters folder named `RatingToStarImageNameConverter` that implements `Xamarin.Forms.IValueConverter`:

```
public class RatingToStarImageNameConverter
    : IValueConverter
{
}
```

2. Next, override the `Convert` and `ConvertBack` methods of `IValueConverter`. In the `Convert` method, we need to check that the value is an integer, and then, based on its value, we convert it to an image filename:

```
public class RatingToStarImageNameConverter
    : IValueConverter
{
    public object Convert (object value, Type targetType,
object parameter, System.Globalization.CultureInfo culture)
    {
        if (value is int) {
            var rating = (int)value;
            if (rating <= 1)
                return "star_1";

            if (rating >= 5)
                return "stars_5";

            return "stars_" + rating;
        }

        return value;
    }

    public object ConvertBack (object value,
Type targetType, object parameter,
System.Globalization.CultureInfo culture)
    {
        throw new NotImplementedException ();
    }
}
```

 The star images used in this code are available in the book's companion code. Be sure to add them to the appropriate place in each of the platform projects.

3. Finally, we need to update the `DetailPage` to use an `Image` view instead of a label to display the entry rating. We will still bind to the same ViewModel property; however, we will use the converter we just created to convert it to an image filename:

```
public DetailPage ()
{
    // ...
```

```
var rating = new Image {
    HorizontalOptions = LayoutOptions.Center
};

rating.SetBinding (Image.SourceProperty, "Entry.Rating",
converter: new RatingToStarImageNameConverter ());

// ...
```

```
Content = mainLayout;
}
```

Now if we run the app and navigate to one of the entries, we will see a much nicer display that immediately causes the rating to standout to the user, as shown in the following screenshot:

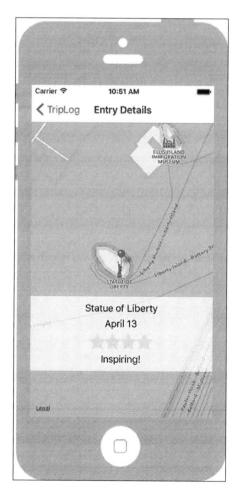

Summary

In this chapter, we leveraged two key concepts in the Xamarin.Forms API to help improve the look and feel and user experience of our TripLog app. With the use of a Custom Renderer, we are able to tap directly into the platform-specific APIs to change the default behavior of Xamarin.Forms controls; and with the use of Value Converters, we are able to alter the appearance of data when it is bound to the user interface. In the next chapter, we are going to connect the TripLog app to an API to get live data.

6
API Data Access

So far in this book, we have worked with static data that is hard-coded directly into the TripLog app itself. However, in the real world, it is rare that an app depends purely on local static data—most mobile apps get their data from a remote data source, typically an API. In some cases, an app may talk to a third party API, for example, that of a social network. Alternatively, developers sometimes create their own API to make data available for their apps. In this chapter, we will create a simple API in the cloud that we can connect to and retrieve data from in the TripLog app.

Here is a quick look at what we will cover in this chapter:

- Creating a live, cloud based backend service and API using Microsoft's Azure App Services platform to store and retrieve TripLog data
- Creating a data access service that handles communication with the API for the TripLog mobile app
- Setting up data caching so the TripLog can work offline

Creating an API with Microsoft Azure App Services

Almost all mobile apps communicate with an API to retrieve and store information. In many cases, as a mobile app developer, you might just have to simply consume an API that already exists. However, if you're building your own service, as opposed to consuming someone else's, you will need to create your own API. There are several ways you can create an API, several places you can host it, and certainly many different languages you can develop it in. For the purposes of this book, we are going to create an API in the cloud using Microsoft Azure App Services. Azure App Services contains many products and features, one of which is called **Mobile Apps** (formally known as Azure Mobile Services).

Azure Mobile Apps provide a very quick and easy way to get a fully functional backend service up and running in a matter of minutes. You can create the backend service using either Node.js or .NET. Because the primary focus of this book is developing a mobile app, I will not spend a lot of time explaining all the granular details of the Azure Mobile Apps Service. So, in this section, we will just cover the basics needed to create a simple, "out-of-the-box" API that we can connect our app to later in this chapter.

In order to follow along with the steps in this chapter, you will need to have an Azure account. If you don't already have an Azure account, you can create one for free at `https://azure.microsoft.com/en-us/pricing/free-trial/`.

Once you have an Azure account, the first thing you need to do is go to the Azure portal in a web browser.

1. Go to `https://portal.azure.com` in a web browser and log in to the Azure portal using your credentials.

2. From the main Azure portal dashboard, click the **+ New** button in the top left corner and select **Web + Mobile**, and then select **Mobile App**.

Figure 1: Setting up a new Mobile App Service in the Microsoft Azure portal

3. Enter a name for your service in the far right **Mobile App** pane.

4. Select your **Subscription**, **Resource Group**, and **App Service Plan** by taking the defaults or creating new ones.

5. Click **Create**.

6. Once your new service has been created, navigate to it from the dashboard.

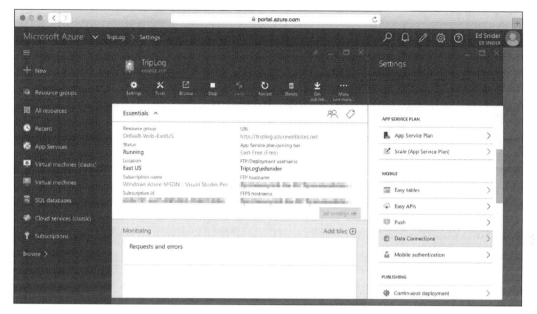

Figure 2: The Mobile App settings pane in the Microsoft Azure portal

7. Next, we need to set up the database that will store the data for the Mobile App Service. Select **Data Connnections** from the **MOBILE** section of the Mobile App settings pane, as shown in *Figure 2*, to set up a new data connection.

Once you have created a new Mobile App in Azure, it will, by default, have no tables or data. Before we can start working with the API, we will need to create a new table that will store our data.

1. Select **Easy tables** from the **MOBILE** section of the Mobile App settings pane.

2. Click the **Add** button. If this is the first table in the service, you may be prompted to configure the service to use **Easy Tables** before creating a new table.

When you configure an App Service to use Easy Tables from within the Azure Portal, it will automatically create a Node.js backend for the service. If you want to use a .NET backend instead, take a look at the documentation at `https://azure.microsoft.com/en-us/documentation/articles/app-service-mobile-xamarin-forms-get-started/#configure-the-server-project`.

3. Name the new table **Entry**, and make sure all the permissions are set to **Allow anonymous access**, as shown in *Figure 3*.

4. Click **OK** and the new Entry table will be added to the list of Easy Tables.

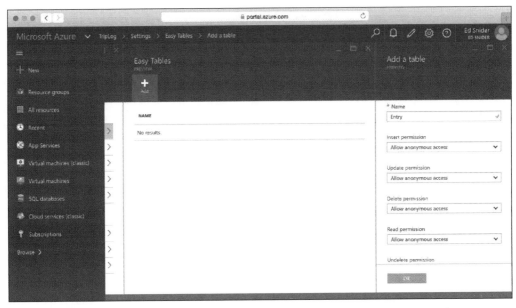

Figure 3: Adding a new data table to the Mobile App in the Microsoft Azure portal

By selecting the **Allow anonymous access** permission, we are making the API available without providing any specific authentication headers in the HTTP request. In the next chapter, we will add authentication to both the API and the mobile app, but for now, we will simply employ anonymous access.

Browsing and adding data

Now that we have created an API in Azure and set up a data table within the service, we can start making calls to the API and getting responses. Before we start making calls to the API from within the TripLog app, we can test the endpoint by making GET and POST HTTP requests to it using the command line or a REST console.

There are several REST consoles to choose from if you don't already have one installed. I typically use either JaSON (`https://github.com/shanebell/JaSON`) or Postman (`http://www.getpostman.com/`). Both are available as Chrome browser apps, making it really easy to install and use them.

> If you don't want to use a REST console, you can use the command line to issue HTTP requests to the API. To do this, use either `curl` in the Terminal on Mac, or `Invoke-RestMethod` in PowerShell on Windows.

1. Using either a REST console or the command line, issue a GET request to the API endpoint for the Entry table using the following URL and header:

   ```
   GET
   https://<your-service-name>.azurewebsites.net/tables/entry
   --header "zumo-api-version:2.0.0"
   ```

2. If everything has been set up properly, we should receive back a 200 status code and an empty collection in the response body, as follows:

   ```
   [ ]
   ```

3. Next, add a new record to the backend service by issuing a POST request to the same API endpoint with an `Entry` JSON object included in the body of the request. The service will automatically create the appropriate columns within the Entry table when we insert the first object:

   ```
   POST
   https://<your-service-name>.azurewebsites.net/tables/entry
   --header "zumo-api-version:2.0.0"
   --data
   {
        "title": "Space Needle",
        "longitude": 47.6204,
        "latitude": -122.3491,
        "date": "2015-07-03T00:00:00.000Z",
        "rating": 5,
        "notes": "Wonderful site to see"
   }
   ```

   We should receive back a 200 status code with the new item we added in the response body.

4. Next, issue another GET response to the `Entry` endpoint:

   ```
   GET
   https://<your-service-name>.azurewebsites.net/tables/entry
   --header "zumo-api-version:2.0.0"
   ```

We should receive back a `200` status code; however, now the response body has a collection containing the new item we added:

```json
[
  {
    "id": "c4a0595d-ac77-4c5b-9d94-f70374e522ab",
    "createdAt": "2015-07-05T21:37:41.946Z",
    "updatedAt": "2015-07-05T21:37:41.977Z",
    "version": "AAAAAAAACBQ=",
    "deleted": false,
    "title": "Space Needle",
    "longitude": 47.6204,
    "latitude": -122.3491,
    "date": "2015-07-03T00:00:00.000Z",
    "rating": 5,
    "notes": "Wonderful site to see"
  }
]
```

Notice that after we added the new record to the backend service, it was automatically given an `id` property, along with a couple of other properties. The `id` property serves as a unique primary key for the record. We will need to update the `TripLogEntry` model in our TripLog app to account for this new property.

5. Add a new `string` property named `Id` to the `TripLogEntry` model class, as follows:

```csharp
public class TripLogEntry
{
    [JsonProperty("id")]
    public string Id { get; set; }
    public string Title { get; set; }
    public double Latitude { get; set; }
    public double Longitude { get; set; }
    public DateTime Date { get; set; }
    public int Rating { get; set; }
    public string Notes { get; set; }
}
```

Now that we have a live backend service that we can communicate with via HTTP, we will update our TripLog app so that it can send requests to the API to add and retrieve log entries.

Creating a base HTTP service

In order for an app to communicate with an API via HTTP, it needs an HTTP library. Because we are using .NET and C# to build a Xamarin.Forms app, we can leverage a library within the .NET Framework called System.Net.Http.HttpClient. The .NET HttpClient provides a mechanism to send and receive data via standard HTTP methods such as GET and POST.

Continuing to keep separation and abstraction key to our app architecture, we will want to keep the specific logic related to the HttpClient separated from the rest of the app. In order to do this, we will write a base service class in our core library that will be responsible for handling HTTP communications in a generic way. This provides a building block for any domain-specific data services we might need to write, for example, a service that is responsible for working with log entries in the API. Any class that will inherit from this class will be able to send HTTP request messages using standard HTTP methods (such as GET, POST, PATCH, DELETE) and get back HTTP response messages without having to deal with HttpClient directly.

As we saw in the preceding section, we are able to post data to the API in the form of JSON; and when we receive data from the API, it's also returned in JSON format. In order for our app to translate its C# models into JSON for use in a HTTP request body, the model will need to be serialized. In contrast, when an HTTP response message is received in JSON, it needs to be deserialized into the appropriate C# model. The most widely used method to do this in .NET software is to use a library called **Json.NET**.

In order to create a base HTTP service, perform the following steps:

1. Add the HttpClient NuGet package to the core library project.
2. Add the Json.NET NuGet package to the core library project and each of the platform-specific projects.
3. Create a new abstract class in the Services folder of the core library named BaseHttpService:

   ```
   public abstract class BaseHttpService
   { }
   ```

4. Add a protected `async` method to the `BaseHttpService` class named `SendRequestAsync<T>` that takes in a `Uri` named `url`, a `HttpMethod` named `httpMethod`, a `IDictionary<string,string>` named `headers`, and an `object` named `requestData`. These four parameters will be used to construct an HTTP request. The `url` parameter is the full URL of the API endpoint for the request. The `httpMethod` optional parameter is used to make the request a GET, POST, and so on. The `headers` optional dictionary parameter is a collection of `string` key/value pairs used to define the header(s) of the request (such as authentication.) Finally, the `requestData` optional parameter is used to pass in an object that will be serialized into JSON and included in the body of POST requests:

```
protected async Task<T> SendRequestAsync<T>(
    Uri url,
    HttpMethod httpMethod = null,
    IDictionary<string, string> headers = null,
    object requestData = null)
{

    var result = default(T);

    // Default to GET
    var method = httpMethod ?? HttpMethod.Get;

    // Serialize request data
    var data = requestData == null
    ? null
    : JsonConvert.SerializeObject (requestData);

    using (var request = new HttpRequestMessage (method, url)) {

        // Add request data to request
        if (data != null)
            request.Content = new StringContent (
            data,
            Encoding.UTF8,
            "application/json");

        // Add headers to request
        if (headers != null)
            foreach (var h in headers)
                request.Headers.Add (h.Key, h.Value);

        // Get response
        using (var handler = new HttpClientHandler ()) {
```

```
                using (var client = new HttpClient (handler)) {
                    using (var response = await client.SendAsync
        (request, HttpCompletionOption.ResponseContentRead)) {
                        var content = response.Content == null
                        ? null
                        : await response
                            .Content
                        .ReadAsStringAsync ();

                        if (response.IsSuccessStatusCode)
                            result = JsonConvert
                            .DeserializeObject<T> (content);
                    }
                }
            }
        }

        return result;
}
```

Now that we have a base HTTP service, we can subclass it with classes that are more specific to our data model, which we will do in the next section.

Creating an API Data Service

Using `BaseHttpService` as a foundation that abstracts away the HTTP request details, we can now begin to create services that leverage it to get responses back from the API in the form of domain-specific models. Specifically, we will create a data service that can be used by the ViewModels to get the `TripLogEntry` objects from the backend service.

We will start off by defining an interface for the data service that can be injected into the ViewModels, ensuring there is no strict dependency on the API or the logic that communicates with it, continuing the pattern we put in place in *Chapter 4, Platform Specific Services and Dependency Injection*.

1. Create a new interface named `ITripLogDataService` in the `Services` folder in the core library:

```
public interface ITripLogDataService
{ }
```

2. Update the `ITripLogDataService` interface with methods to get, update, and delete `TripLogEntry` objects:

```
public interface ITripLogDataService
{
    Task<IList<TripLogEntry>> GetEntriesAsync ();
    Task<TripLogEntry> GetEntryAsync (string id);
    Task<TripLogEntry> AddEntryAsync (TripLogEntry entry);
    Task<TripLogEntry> UpdateEntryAsync (TripLogEntry entry);
    Task RemoveEntryAsync (TripLogEntry entry);
}
```

Next, we need to create an implementation of this interface that will also subclass `BaseHttpService` so that it has access to our `HttpClient` implementation.

3. Create a new class named `TripLogApiDataService` in the `Services` folder in the core library:

```
public class TripLogApiDataService
    : BaseHttpService, ITripLogDataService
{ }
```

4. Add two private properties to the `TripLogApiDataService` class: a `Uri` and an `IDictionary<string, string>`, to store the base URL and headers respectively, to be used for all requests:

```
public class TripLogApiDataService
    : BaseHttpService, ITripLogDataService
{
    readonly Uri _baseUri;
    readonly IDictionary<string, string> _headers;
}
```

5. Update the `TripLogApiDataService` constructor to take in a `Uri` parameter and set the private `_baseUri` and `_headers` properties:

```
public class TripLogApiDataService
    : BaseHttpService, ITripLogDataService
{
    readonly Uri _baseUri;
    readonly IDictionary<string, string> _headers;

    public TripLogApiDataService (Uri baseUri)
    {
        _baseUri = baseUri;
        _headers = new Dictionary<string, string> ();
```

```
        // TODO: Add header with Authentication-based token in
chapter 7
        _headers.Add ("zumo-api-version", "2.0.0");
    }
}
```

6. Finally, implement the members of ITripLogDataService using the
    SendRequestAsync<T> base class method:

```
public class TripLogApiDataService
    : BaseHttpService, ITripLogDataService
{
    readonly Uri _baseUri;
    readonly IDictionary<string, string> _headers;

    // ...

    #region ITripLogDataService implementation

    public async Task<IList<TripLogEntry>> GetEntriesAsync ()
    {
        var url = new Uri (_baseUri, "/tables/entry");
        var response = await SendRequestAsync<TripLogEntry[]>
(url, HttpMethod.Get, _headers);
        return response;
    }

    public async Task<TripLogEntry> GetEntryAsync (string id)
    {
        var url = new Uri (_baseUri, string.Format ("/tables/
entry/{0}", id));
        var response = await SendRequestAsync<TripLogEntry> (url,
HttpMethod.Get, _headers);
        return response;
    }

    public async Task<TripLogEntry> AddEntryAsync (TripLogEntry
entry)
    {
        var url = new Uri (_baseUri, "/tables/entry");
        var response = await SendRequestAsync<TripLogEntry> (url,
HttpMethod.Post, _headers, entry);
        return response;
    }
```

```
        public async Task<TripLogEntry> UpdateEntryAsync (TripLogEntry
entry)
        {
            var url = new Uri (_baseUri, string.Format ("/tables/
entry/{0}", entry.Id));
            var response = await SendRequestAsync<TripLogEntry>(url,
new HttpMethod("PATCH"), _headers, entry);
            return response;
        }

        public async Task RemoveEntryAsync (TripLogEntry entry)
        {
            var url = new Uri (_baseUri, string.Format ("/tables/
entry/{0}", entry.Id));
            var response = await SendRequestAsync<TripLogEntry>(url,
HttpMethod.Delete, _headers);
        }

        #endregion
}
```

Each method in this TripLog service calls the `SendRequestAsync` method on the base class passing in the API route, the appropriate `HttpMethod`, and the `zumo-api-version` header that we used in the first section. The `Add` and `Update` methods also pass in a `TripLogEntry` object that will be serialized and added to the HTTP request message content. In the next chapter, we will implement authentication with the API and update this service to pass in an authentication based token in the header.

Updating the TripLog app ViewModels

Using the API and data service we created, we can now update the ViewModels in the app to use live data instead of the local, hard-coded data they currently use. We will continue to leverage the patterns we put in place in previous chapters to ensure our ViewModels remain testable and do not have any specific dependencies on the Azure API or even the HTTP communication logic.

1. First, update the `TripLogCoreModule` in the core library to register our `ITripLogDataService` implementation into the IoC:

```
public class TripLogCoreModule : NinjectModule
{
    public override void Load ()
    {
        // ViewModels
        Bind<MainViewModel> ().ToSelf ();
```

```
            Bind<DetailViewModel> ().ToSelf ();
            Bind<NewEntryViewModel> ().ToSelf ();

            // Core Services
            var tripLogService = new TripLogApiDataService (new
        Uri("https://<your-service-name>.azurewebsites.net"));

            Bind<ITripLogDataService> ()
                .ToMethod (x => tripLogService)
                .InSingletonScope ();
        }
    }
```

2. Next, update the `MainViewModel` constructor to take an `ITripLogDataService` parameter, which will be provided automatically via dependency injection:

```
readonly ITripLogDataService _tripLogService;

public MainViewModel (
    INavService navService,
    ITripLogDataService tripLogService)
    : base (navService)
{
    _tripLogService = tripLogService;

    LogEntries = new ObservableCollection<TripLogEntry> ();
}
```

3. Then, we need to update the `LoadEntries` method in `MainViewModel`, replacing the three second delay and hard-coded data population with a call to the live TripLog API via the current `ITripLogDataService` that was injected into the ViewModel's constructor:

```
async Task LoadEntries()
{
    if (IsBusy)
        return;

    IsBusy = true;

    try
    {
        var entries = await _tripLogService.GetEntriesAsync ();

        LogEntries = new ObservableCollection<TripLogEntry>
    (entries);
```

```
    }
    finally {
        IsBusy = false;
    }
}
```

No other changes to `MainViewModel` are required. Now, when the app is launched, instead of the hard-coded data loading, you will see the items stored in the Azure backend service database.

Now, we need to update the `NewEntryViewModel` so that when we add a new entry, it is actually saved to the Azure backend through the data service.

1. Update the `NewEntryViewModel` constructor to take an `ITripLogDataService` parameter:

   ```
   readonly ITripLogDataService _tripLogService;

   public NewEntryViewModel (
       INavService navService,
       ILocationService locService,
       ITripLogDataService tripLogService)
       : base (navService)
   {
       _locService = locService;
       _tripLogService = tripLogService;

       Date = DateTime.Today;
       Rating = 1;
   }
   ```

2. Then, we need to update the SaveCommand execute `Action` method to call the `AddEntryAsync` method on the data service:

   ```
   async Task ExecuteSaveCommand()
   {
       if (IsBusy)
           return;

       IsBusy = true;

       var newItem = new TripLogEntry {
           Title = this.Title,
           Latitude = this.Latitude,
           Longitude = this.Longitude,
           Date = this.Date,
   ```

```
            Rating = this.Rating,
            Notes = this.Notes
    };

    try
    {
        await _tripLogService.AddEntryAsync (newItem);
        await NavService.GoBack ();
    }
    finally {
        IsBusy = false;
    }
}
```

Now, if we launch the app, navigate to the new entry page, fill out the form, and click **Save**, the log entry will be sent to the TripLog backend service and saved in the database.

Offline data caching

Mobile apps have several benefits over web apps, one of which is the ability to operate offline and maintain offline data. There are a couple of reasons why offline data is important to a mobile app. First of all, you cannot guarantee your app will always have a network connection and the ability to directly connect to live data; so, supporting "offline" allows users to use the app, even if only for limited use cases, when they are operating with limited or no connectivity. Second, users expect mobile apps to offer high performance, specifically quick access to data without having to wait. By maintaining an offline cache, an app can present a user with data immediately while it's busy retrieving a fresh data set, providing perceived performance to the user. It is important that when the cache updates, the user receives that updated data automatically so that they are always seeing the latest data possible, depending on specific use cases of course.

There are several ways of implementing a data cache in a mobile app, all depending on the size and complexity of the data that needs to be stored. In most cases, storing the cache in a local database using SQLite is the best approach.

In this chapter, we will update the TripLog app to maintain a cache of log entries and keep the cache in sync with the live API as data is received from Azure backend service. The data cache will be stored in a SQLite database, but to ease the implementation, we will use an open source library called **Akavache**. Akavache provides not only caching capabilities, but also a very easy to use API to update the cache to handle many different scenarios.

> For the purposes of this book and the TripLog sample application, we will only be using a small subset of the Akavache features. For a closer look at the Akavache library and all of its capabilities, check it out on GitHub at `https://github.com/akavache/Akavache`.

Adding the Akavache library

Like most libraries that we have used throughout this book, the Akavache library can be obtained via NuGet. First, add a reference to the library, including all of its dependencies to the core library project and the platform-specific projects.

Next, we need to add Akavache to our IoC container so that it can be injected into our ViewModels. Akavache comes with some static variables that make it very easy to use; however, we want to instead instantiate our own instance and add it to the IoC to maintain separation.

```
Bind<Akavache.IBlobCache> ().ToConstant (Akavache.BlobCache.
LocalMachine);
```

Maintaining an offline data cache

Currently, the TripLog app's `MainViewModel` calls the `TripLogApiDataService` to get its data directly from the live API. As mentioned at the beginning of this chapter, in the event of little or no connectivity, the TripLog app will fail to display any log entries. With a few minor modifications to the `MainViewModel`, we can set it up to use the Akavache library to retrieve log entries from a local cache and also to refresh that cache with any changes in the data set once a connection with live API has succeeded.

First, update the `MainViewModel` constructor to require an instance of `Akavache.IBlobCache`, which will be injected via our Ninject implementation from *Chapter 4, Platform Specific Services and Dependency Injection*:

```
readonly IBlobCache _cache;

// ...

public MainViewModel (INavService navService,
   ITripLogDataService tripLogService,
   IBlobCache cache)
   : base (navService)
{
   _tripLogService = tripLogService;
```

```
    _cache = cache;

    LogEntries = new ObservableCollection<TripLogEntry> ();
}
```

Next, we need to modify the logic in the `LoadEntries` method to tie into the local offline cache. To do this, we will leverage an extension method in Akavache called `GetAndFetchLatest`. This method actually performs two functions. First, it immediately returns cached data, given a specific key (in our case, `entries`.) Second, it makes a call to the API based on the given `Func` and updates the cache for the given specific key. Because it is performing two functions, it will ultimately return twice. In order to handle this, and because it is returning an `IObservable`, we can use the `ObservableExtensions` `Subscribe` extension method to handle each return as it occurs. In the `Subscribe` extension method, we will update the `LogEntries` `ObservableCollection` property on the `MainViewModel` based on what is either returned from the cache or from the subsequent API call, if successful:

```
public override async Task Init ()
{
    LoadEntries ();
}

void LoadEntries()
{
    if (IsBusy)
        return;

    IsBusy = true;

    try
    {
        // Load from local cache and then immediately load from API
        _cache.GetAndFetchLatest("entries",
            async () => await _tripLogService.GetEntriesAsync())
            .Subscribe(entries => {
                LogEntries =
                new ObservableCollection<TripLogEntry>(entries);
            });
    }
    finally {
        IsBusy = false;
    }
}
```

Notice that, because we're calling GetAndFetchLatest and using the Subscribe method, the LoadEntries method is no longer async.

The first time the app is launched with this code, the cache will be populated. On any subsequent launches of the app, you should notice that data appears immediately as the view is constructed. If you add an item to the backend service database, and then launch the app again, you should see the new item fall into place after a couple of seconds.

Summary

In this chapter, we created a live API from scratch using Azure App Services. We then created a data service within our app to handle communication between the app and the API. Then, by adding a reference to this service to our ViewModels, we quickly transformed the app from using static data to using live data from our new API. Finally, we set up offline data caching. In the next chapter, we will add authentication to our API and update the app with sign in capabilities.

7
Authentication

Here is a quick look at what we'll cover in this chapter:

- How to add authentication to Azure Mobile Apps
- How to use the Xamarin.Auth component to easily perform OAuth and securely communicate with the API
- How to update the TripLog app with a sign in page

Adding identity and authentication to Azure Mobile Apps

In the previous chapter, we set up a new, live backend service hosted in Microsoft Azure. The service contains a single table, Entry, which houses all log entries for our TripLog app. Currently, the Entry table is available anonymously. In this section, we are going to change the permissions on the Entry table to require each request to contain an access token associated with an authenticated user.

Setting up permissions

In order to enforce authentication to access our backend service, we need to make a simple configuration change to the Entry table.

1. Select your **TripLog** Mobile App in the Azure portal.
2. Click **Settings**.

3. Click **Easy Tables** in the **MOBILE** section of the **Settings** pane and then select the **Entry** table, as shown in the following screenshot:

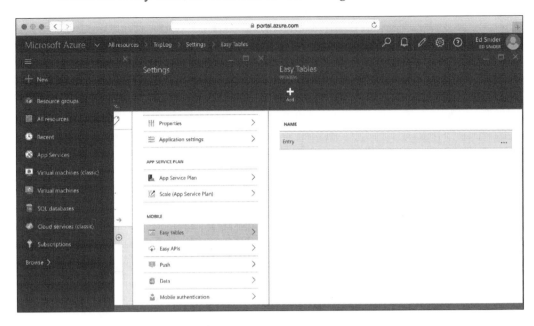

4. Click the **Change permission** button, as shown in the following screenshot:

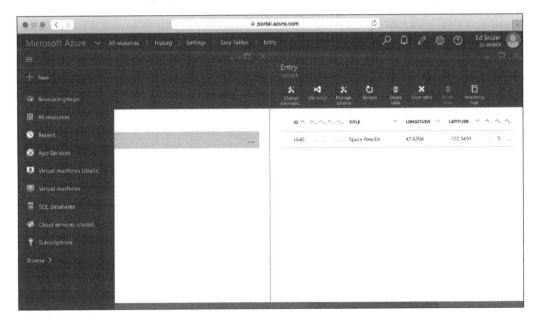

5. Change each of the table permissions to **Authenticated access only**. Then, click the **Save** button at the top of the pane.

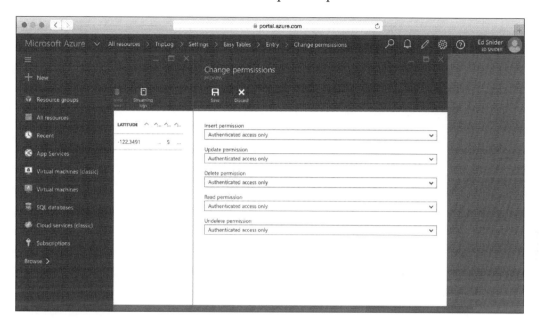

Now, any attempt to call the API endpoints, as we did in the previous chapter, will result in a 401 response. For example, using either a REST console or the command line, issue a GET request to the API endpoint for the **Entry** table using the following URL and header:

```
GET
https://<your-service-name>.azurewebsites.net/tables/entry
--header "zumo-api-version:2.0.0"
```

You should now get back the following response message, since we are not providing any valid authentication token in the request:

```
You must be logged in to use this application
```

In the next section, we will set up Facebook as an identity provider in our Azure backend service so that we can obtain a user specific access token that can be used in the request headers, allowing us to get back a successful response.

Setting up an identity provider

There are a couple of approaches to handle identity and authentication in Azure. You can set up the Azure Mobile App service to use Facebook, Twitter, Microsoft Account, Google, or even Azure Active Directory as a trusted identity provider. You can also create your own custom identity provider if you want to use account data stored in your database instead of one of the social providers. You can use one of these options or a combination of several of them — they will all provide an access token that can be used by your mobile app to communicate with your API on behalf of your users. In this section, we are going to use only one provider — Facebook.

In order to use a social network as an identity provider, you will need to have an app/client ID and app secret. These keys can be obtained directly from the identity provider by setting up an app for OAuth, typically in their developer portal. Once you have obtained the app/client ID and secret, you can configure the authentication settings for the backend service.

1. Select your **TripLog** mobile app in the Azure portal.
2. Select **Settings**.
3. Select **Authentication / Authorization**, as shown in the following screenshot:

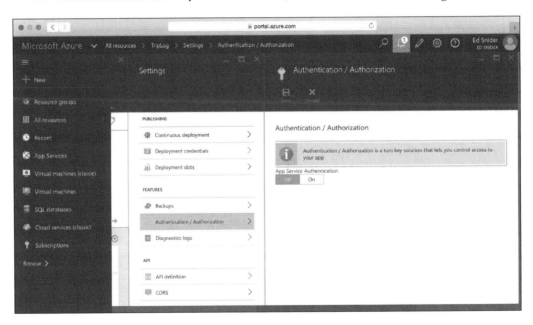

4. Switch the **App Service Authentication** toggle to **On**, as shown in the following screenshot:

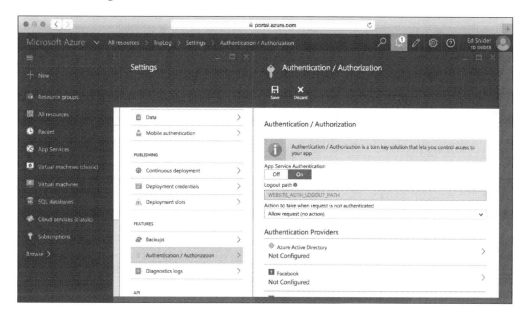

5. Select **Facebook**.

6. Provide your Facebook **App ID** and **App Secret** and click the **OK** button at the bottom of the **Facebook** pane, as shown in the following screenshot:

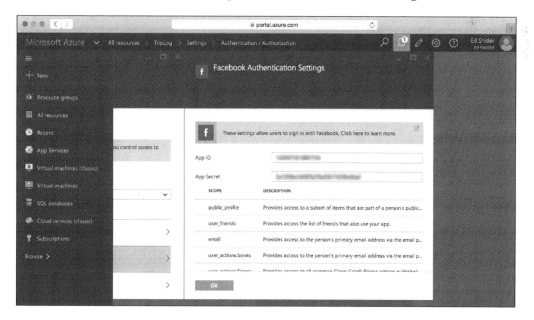

7. Click the **Save** button at the top of the **Authentication/Authorization** pane.

8. Next, you need to add the OAuth redirect **URI (Uniform Resource Identifier)** for your service within the app setting of the identity provider. The redirect URI will depend on the identity provider using the following format: `https://<your-service-name>.azurewebsites.net/.auth/login/<identity-proider>/callback`. Replace `<your-service-name>` with the name of your Azure Mobile App, and `<identity-provider>` with either `facebook`, `twitter`, `microsoftaccount`, `google`, or `aad`, depending on which identity provider you are using.

> Setting up an app for OAuth is different for each provider, and the Azure Mobile Apps documentation has outlined the steps in detail for each, as follows:
>
> Facebook: `https://azure.microsoft.com/en-us/documentation/articles/app-service-mobile-how-to-configure-facebook-authentication/`
>
> Twitter: `https://azure.microsoft.com/en-us/documentation/articles/app-service-mobile-how-to-configure-twitter-authentication/`
>
> Microsoft Account: `https://azure.microsoft.com/en-us/documentation/articles/app-service-mobile-how-to-configure-microsoft-authentication/`
>
> Google: `https://azure.microsoft.com/en-us/documentation/articles/app-service-mobile-how-to-configure-google-authentication/`
>
> Azure Active Directory: `https://azure.microsoft.com/en-us/documentation/articles/app-service-mobile-how-to-configure-active-directory-authentication/`

Once you have set everything up on the identity provider side and provided the keys in the Azure portal, you can test it out in your internet browser by going to `https://<your-service-name>.azurewebsites.net/.auth/login/facebook`.

If it is all set up correctly, you should see the login prompt for the identity provider. After providing your credentials, you should be prompted to give your app permission to use your account.

If you observe the URL in the browser address bar after clicking **OK**, you should see the redirected URL appended with a token value in the form of a URL encoded JSON object. We can then take the value of the `authenticationToken` key in that JSON object and use it in a request to our API to confirm that we get back a successful response.

In either a REST console or the command line, issue the same GET request that we did in the preceding section, but this time, add a new header named x-zumo-auth, and use the value from authenticationToken in the JSON object returned in the redirect URI as the x-zumo-auth header value:

```
GET
https://<your-service-name>.azurewebsites.net/tables/entry
--header "zumo-api-version:2.0.0"
--header "x-zumo-auth:<your-authentication-token>"
```

If everything has been set up correctly, you should get back a response containing all of the Entry objects in Azure backend service.

In the next section, we will update the TripLog app with a Facebook authentication page to get an access token that can be stored and used by the app to communicate with the API.

Creating an authentication service

Now that we have enabled our backend service with Facebook authentication, the app as it is from the previous chapter will fail to load content. In this section, we will update the app to authenticate users with Facebook via OAuth and obtain an access token from Azure that can be used in subsequent API calls by the TripLogApiDataService.

As in the previous chapter, instead of using the Azure Mobile Apps SDK, we will directly call the REST endpoints behind the SDK to better understand the approach to authenticate to an API in a more generic way. In order to do this, we will first make an OAuth call to Facebook, obtaining a Facebook token. We will then pass that token to an Azure Mobile App endpoint, where it is validated using the Facebook app ID and secret that was added to the service's configuration in Azure to finally receive the access token needed to make calls to the API table endpoints.

Performing OAuth in a mobile app requires a certain set of platform-specific capabilities; so, we will need to follow the same pattern that we did in earlier chapters, as follows:

1. First, create a new interface named IAuthService in the Services folder in the core library:

```
public interface IAuthService
{ }
```

2. Update the `IAuthService` interface with a single method that takes in all the key components of a standard OAuth call as its parameters:

```
public interface IAuthService
{
    Task SignInAsync (string clientId,
        Uri authUrl,
        Uri callbackUrl,
        Action<string> tokenCallback,
        Action<string> errorCallback);
}
```

The two callback `Action` parameters provide a way to handle both success and failure OAuth responses.

Next, we need to create an implementation of this interface. Just as we did with the geo-location service in *Chapter 4, Platform Specific Services and Dependency Injection,* we will leverage a Xamarin Component to create the actual platform-specific implementation for `IAuthService`. The Xamarin.Auth Component provides an easy to use cross-platform API to conduct OAuth in Xamarin mobile apps.

1. Add the Xamarin.Auth Xamarin Component to each of the platform projects (that is, TripLog.iOS and TripLog.Droid) by right-clicking on the `Components` folder.

2. Next, create a new class named `AuthService` in the `Services` folder in the TripLog.iOS project:

```
public class AuthService : IAuthService
{ }
```

3. Next, provide the implementation for the `SignInAsync` method:

```
public class AuthService : IAuthService
{
    public async Task SignInAsync (string clientId,
        Uri authUrl,
        Uri callbackUrl,
        Action<string> tokenCallback,
        Action<string> errorCallback)
    {
        var auth = new OAuth2Authenticator (clientId,
            string.Empty,
            authUrl,
            callbackUrl);

        auth.AllowCancel = true;
```

```
                var controller = auth.GetUI();
                await UIApplication.SharedApplication
                    .KeyWindow
                    .RootViewController
                    .PresentViewControllerAsync(controller, true);

                auth.Completed += (s, e) =>
                {
                    controller.DismissViewController(true, null);
                    if (e.Account != null && e.IsAuthenticated)
                    {
                        if (tokenCallback != null)
                            tokenCallback(e.Account
                                .Properties["access_token"]);
                    }
                    else
                    {
                        if (errorCallback != null)
                            errorCallback("Not authenticated");
                    }
                };

                auth.Error += (s, e) =>
                {
                    controller.DismissViewController(true, null);
                    if (errorCallback != null)
                        errorCallback(e.Message);
                };
            }
        }
```

4. Finally, update the `TripLogPlatformModule` in each platform-specific project to register its `IAuthService` implementation into the IoC:

```
public class TripLogPlatformModule : NinjectModule
{
    public override void Load ()
    {
        Bind<ILocationService> ()
            .To<LocationService> ()
            .InSingletonScope ();

        Bind<IAuthService> ()
            .To<AuthService> ()
            .InSingletonScope ();
    }
}
```

The IAuthService provides a way to perform OAuth against Facebook, which gives us a Facebook authentication token, but we still need a way to pass that Facebook specific token to our API to get back an Azure authenticated access token that we can use in our requests. Azure Mobile Apps provide an endpoint that takes an identity provider-specific token, and in return, provides back an Azure-specific token. In order to use this endpoint, we just need to update our TripLog data service with a new method, as follows:

1. First, create a new model class named TripLogApiAuthToken. As we saw in the preceding section, the response from the /.auth/login/facebook endpoint is a JSON object containing a user object and an authenticationToken object; so, this TripLogApiAuthToken model will represent that structure so that we can deserialize the response and use the access token for future calls to the TripLog backend service:

```
public class TripLogApiUser
{
    public string UserId { get; set; }
}
public class TripLogApiAuthToken
{
    public TripLogApiUser User { get; set; }
    public string AuthenticationToken { get; set; }
}
```

2. Next, add a new method to the ITripLogDataService interface named GetAuthTokenAsync that returns an object of the TripLogApiAuthToken type we just created:

```
public interface ITripLogDataService
{
    Task<TripLogApiAuthToken> GetAuthTokenAsync(string idProvider,
string idProviderToken);
    Task<IList<TripLogEntry>> GetEntriesAsync ();
    Task<TripLogEntry> GetEntryAsync (string id);
    Task<TripLogEntry> AddEntryAsync (TripLogEntry entry);
    Task<TripLogEntry> UpdateEntryAsync (TripLogEntry entry);
    Task RemoveEntryAsync (TripLogEntry entry);
}
```

Notice the idProvider parameter, which allows this method to be used for Azure social identity providers beyond just Facebook.

3. Next, update the `TripLogApiDataService` to include the implementation for the `GetAuthTokenAsync` method that we just added to `ITripLogDataService`. The method needs to make a POST call to the `/.auth/login/facebook` endpoint with the access token received from the OAuth response in the request body. The service endpoint expects the token in the body to be associated with a key named `access_token`. Because our base HTTP service handles serializing the message body data for us, we can simply create a `struct` to house the token that will be passed to the endpoint:

```
public class TripLogApiDataService
    : BaseHttpService, ITripLogDataService
{
    readonly Uri _baseUri;
    IDictionary<string, string> _headers;

    // ...

    struct IdProviderToken
    {
        [JsonProperty("access_token")]
        public string AccessToken { get; set; }
    }

    public async Task<TripLogApiAuthToken>
GetAuthTokenAsync(string idProvider, string idProviderToken)
    {
        var token = new IdProviderToken {
            AccessToken = idProviderToken
        };

        var url = new Uri (_baseUri,
            string.Format (".auth/login/{0}", idProvider));

        var response = await SendRequestAsync<TripLogApiAuthToken>
(url, HttpMethod.Post, _headers, token);

        // Update this service with the new auth token
        if (response != null) {
            var authToken = response.AuthenticationToken;
            _headers["x-zumo-auth"] = authToken;
        }

        return response;
    }

    // ...
}
```

4. Finally, we need to update the `TripLogApiDataService` constructor with a string parameter named `authToken`. In the `GetAuthTokenAsync` method, we update the `_headers` property within the service with token we received from the backend. However, we also need to be able to set the `_headers` property from the constructor so that we can initialize the service with a token, if one already exists (for instance, if a token was persisted in the app's settings after signing in).

```
public TripLogApiDataService (Uri baseUri,
    string authToken)
{
    _baseUri = baseUri;
    _headers = new Dictionary<string, string> ();

    _headers.Add ("zumo-api-version", "2.0.0");
    _headers.Add ("x-zumo-auth", authToken);
}
```

Adding a sign in page

In order to add sign in capabilities to our app, we need to create a new Page and a new ViewModel. The ViewModel will be pretty straightforward, containing just a single command that handles signing in to Facebook via the `IAuthService`, passing the received Facebook token to the Azure backend service through the `ITripLogDataService`, and then storing the Azure access token in local settings.

There are a couple of ways to tap into the local storage platform-specific APIs to store settings. One way is to roll your own, similar to how we did the location service: creating a core interface that is implemented uniquely per platform. Another alternative is to leverage a *plugin* or other third party component that has been published. In this section, we will use a plugin called **Settings Plugin for Xamarin and Windows**, available on NuGet as **Xam. Plugins.Settings** by James Montemagno. There are also several other types of plugins made available by members of the Xamarin community at `https://github.com/xamarin/plugins`.

1. Add the Xam.Plugins.Settings NuGet package to the core library and each of the platform-specific projects, and update the Settings helper class in the core library according to the package's readme file to include a string setting named TripLogApiAuthToken.

2. Create a new class that inherits from `BaseViewModel` named `SignInViewModel` in the ViewModels folder in the core library:

```
public class SignInViewModel : BaseViewModel
{ }
```

3. Update the `SignInViewModel` with a constructor that takes in an `INavService`, `IAuthService`, and `ITripLogDataService` parameter:

```
public class SignInViewModel : BaseViewModel
{
    readonly IAuthService _authService;
    readonly ITripLogDataService _tripLogService;

    public SignInViewModel (INavService navService,
IAuthService authService,
ITripLogDataService tripLogService)
        :base(navService)
    {
        _authService = authService;
        _tripLogService = tripLogService;
    }
}
```

4. Next, add a new `ICommand` property named `SignInCommand` to the `SignInViewModel` along with its execute `Action`:

```
public class SignInViewModel : BaseViewModel
{
    // ...

    ICommand _signInCommand;
    public ICommand SignInCommand {
        get {
            return _signInCommand
?? (_signInCommand = new Command (async () => await
ExecuteSignInCommand ()));
        }
    }

    async Task ExecuteSignInCommand()
    {
        // TODO: Update with your Facebook Client Id
        await _authService.SignInAsync (
"YOUR_FACEBOOK_CLIENTID",
            new Uri ("https://m.facebook.com/dialog/oauth"),
```

```
            new Uri ("https://triplog.azurewebsites.net/.auth/
    login/facebook/callback"),
                tokenCallback: async t => {

                    // Use Facebook token to get Azure auth token
                    var response = await _tripLogService.
    GetAuthTokenAsync ("facebook", t);

                    // Save auth token in local settings
                    Helpers.Settings.TripLogApiAuthToken = response.
    AuthenticationToken;

                    // Navigate to Main
                    await NavService.NavigateTo<MainViewModel> ();
                    await NavService.RemoveLastView ();
                },
                errorCallback: e => {
                    // TODO: Handle invalid authentication here
                });
        }
    }
```

5. Override the `BaseViewModel Init` method to clear the navigation back stack anytime the `SignInViewModel` is loaded:

```
public override async Task Init ()
{
    await NavService.ClearBackStack ();
}
```

6. Update the `TripLogCoreModule` to add `SignInViewModel` to the IoC container:

```
public class TripLogCoreModule : NinjectModule
{
    public override void Load ()
    {
        // ViewModels
        Bind<SignInViewModel> ().ToSelf();
        Bind<MainViewModel> ().ToSelf ();
        Bind<DetailViewModel> ().ToSelf ();
        Bind<NewEntryViewModel> ().ToSelf ();

        // ...
    }
}
```

7. Update the `TripLogCoreModule` to account for the updated
   `TripLogApiDataService` constructor and pass in the auth token
   stored in local settings:

```
var tripLogService = new TripLogApiDataService (
new Uri("https://<your-service-name>.azurewebsites.net"),
Helpers.Settings.TripLogApiAuthToken);
```

Next, we need to create the actual sign in page, which we will use with the
`SignInViewModel` as its data context.

1. Create a new page in the `Views` folder in the core library named `SignInPage`:

```
public class SignInPage : ContentPage
{ }
```

2. Update the constructor of the `SignInPage` to add a button that is bound to
   `SignInViewModel`'s `SignInCommand`:

```
public class SignInPage : ContentPage
{
    public SignInPage ()
    {
        Padding = 20;

        var facebookButton = new Button {
            BackgroundColor = Color.FromHex("#455c9f"),
            TextColor = Color.White,
            Text = "Sign in with Facebook"
        };
        facebookButton.SetBinding (Button.CommandProperty,
"SignInCommand");

        var mainLayout = new StackLayout {
            VerticalOptions = LayoutOptions.Center,
            Children = { facebookButton }
        };

        Content = mainLayout;
    }
}
```

3. Next, register the `SignInPage` and `SignInViewModel` mapping in the
   navigation service in the `TripLogNavModule`:

```
public class TripLogNavModule : NinjectModule
{
    // ...
```

```
public override void Load ()
{
    var navService = new XamarinFormsNavService ();
    navService.XamarinFormsNav = _xfNav;

    // Register view mappings
    navService.RegisterViewMapping (typeof(SignInViewModel),
typeof(SignInPage));
    navService.RegisterViewMapping (typeof(MainViewModel),
typeof(MainPage));
    navService.RegisterViewMapping (typeof(DetailViewModel),
typeof(DetailPage));
    navService.RegisterViewMapping (typeof(NewEntryViewModel),
typeof(NewEntryPage));

    Bind<INavService> ().ToMethod (x => navService)
            .InSingletonScope ();
}
}
```

Finally, we need to make two minor adjustments to the app so that users will go directly to the SignInPage if an auth token does not exist in local settings.

1. First, add a public bool property to the App class that indicates if an auth token is present by checking the Settings helper class:

```
public bool IsSignedIn {
    get {
        return
            !string.IsNullOrWhiteSpace (Helpers.Settings.
TripLogApiAuthToken);
    }
}
```

2. Next, update the Init method of the MainViewModel to forward the user to the SignInViewModel if the IsSignedIn property is false:

```
public override async Task Init ()
{
    if (!((App)Application.Current).IsSignedIn)
        await NavService.NavigateTo<SignInViewModel> ();
    else
        LoadEntries ();
}
```

Now, when the app is launched for the first time and an auth token is not present in the local settings, you will see the `SignInPage`. Clicking the sign in button will launch the Xamarin.Auth dialog prompting for Facebook credentials and permission to grant access to the TripLog app, as shown in the following screenshots. Upon successfully authenticating with Facebook, you should be automatically brought to the `MainPage` and the list of the `Entry` objects will be loaded from the API.

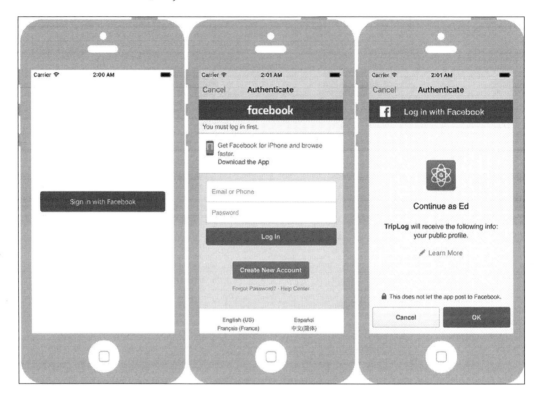

Summary

In this chapter, we updated the Azure backend service we created in the previous chapter with Facebook provided identity. We also updated the API data service in the TripLog app to authenticate its HTTP API requests with a user-specific auth token provided by Azure Mobile Apps service given a valid Facebook access token. Finally, we added a sign in page and updated the app to automatically route the user to the sign in page if an auth token isn't found in local settings. In the next, chapter we are going to create unit tests and automated UI tests for our TripLog app.

8
Testing

Throughout the book, we have implemented patterns and best practices with the intention of separating the layers of our TripLog app, making it easier to maintain and test. In this chapter, we will write tests for our business logic by unit testing ViewModels, and we will write tests for our UI with automated UI testing.

Here is a quick look at what we will cover in this chapter:

- Unit testing with NUnit
- Automated UI testing with the Xamarin.UITest framework

Unit testing

We will start by testing the business logic in the TripLog app. We will do this by creating a new unit test project in our solution that will be responsible for testing our ViewModels.

There are many options and libraries to create unit tests in .NET. By default, Xamarin Studio leverages the popular NUnit framework for performing unit tests.

In order to create a unit test project, perform the following steps:

1. Create a new solution folder named `Tests`. While this is not required, it helps keep any testing-related projects organized within the overall solution. To add a new solution folder in Xamarin Studio, simply right click on the solution, go to **Add** and click on **Add Solution Folder**, as seen in *Figure 1*:

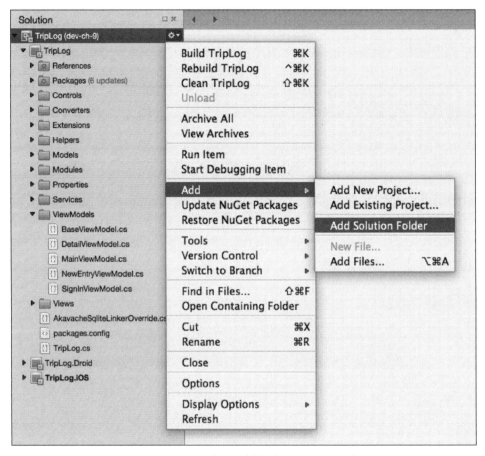

Figure 1 Creating a new solution folder for testing related projects

2. Next, create a new NUnit project in the new `Tests` solution folder and name it `TripLog.Tests`.

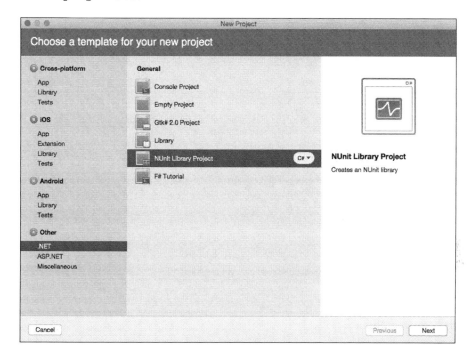

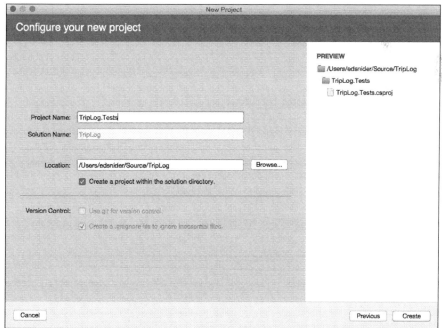

By default, the new NUnit project will contain a file named **Test.cs**. You can safely delete this file, as we will create new ones that are specific to each of our ViewModels in the next section.

Testing ViewModels

When unit testing ViewModels, it is best to break the tests into individual test classes that represent each ViewModel, resulting in a one-to-one relationship between ViewModel classes and the unit test classes that test their logic.

In order to test our ViewModels, we will need to reference them within the unit tests project.

Add a reference to the TripLog core library project to the `TripLog.Tests` project.

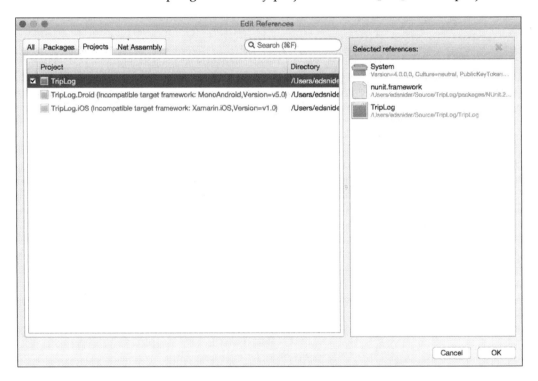

We will start by creating a set of unit tests for `DetailViewModel`:

1. Create a new empty class named `DetailViewModelTests` within the new `TripLog.Tests` project.

2. Next, update the `DetailViewModelTests` class with a `TestFixture` attribute:

```
[TestFixture]
public class DetailViewModelTests
{ }
```

3. Next, create a test `Setup` function in the `DetailViewModelTests` class:

```
[TestFixture]
public class DetailViewModelTests
{
    [SetUp]
    public void Setup()
    {

    }
}
```

This `Setup` method will be responsible for creating new instances of our ViewModel for each of the tests within the class by ensuring that each test is run with a clean, known state of the ViewModel under test.

In order to create a new instance of a ViewModel, we need to provide it with the instances of the services required by its constructor. During runtime, these are automatically provided via dependency injection, but in the case of the unit tests, we need to provide them manually. We have a couple of options here; we can create new mock versions of our services and pass them into the ViewModel's constructor. This requires providing a mock implementation for each method in the service's interface, which can be time-consuming and it causes additional code maintenance. We can also use a mocking library to create mocks of the services, and we can pass these mocks into the ViewModel's constructor. The mocking library provides a much cleaner approach that is also less fragile. Additionally, most mocking libraries will provide a way to specify how methods or properties should return data in a much cleaner way without actually having to implement them ourselves. I like to use Moq (available on NuGet)—a very popular mocking library for .NET applications—to handle mocking for my unit tests.

In order to initialize the ViewModel with mocked services, perform the following steps:

1. Add a reference to the `Moq` NuGet package to the `TripLog.Tests` project.

2. Next, within the `Setup` method, create a new instance of `DetailViewModel`. Use the `Moq` library to create a mock instance of `INavService` to pass in when instantiating `DetailViewModel`:

```
[TestFixture]
public class DetailViewModelTests
{
    DetailViewModel _vm;

    [SetUp]
    public void Setup()
    {
        var navMock = new Mock<INavService> ().Object;
        _vm = new DetailViewModel (navMock);
    }
}
```

Now that we have a setup function defined, we can create an actual test method. This ViewModel does not do much beyond initialization. Therefore, we will just test the `Init` method to make sure that the ViewModel is properly initialized when its `Init` method is called. The success criteria for this particular test will be that once `Init` is called, the `Entry` property of the ViewModel will be set to the value provided in the `Init` method's parameter.

In order to create a test for the ViewModel's `Init` method, perform the following steps:

1. Create a new method in `DetailViewModelTests` named `Init_ParameterProvided_EntryIsSet`, and decorate it with an NUnit `[Test]` attribute. Each test method that we create will follow the **Arrange-Act-Assert** pattern:

```
[TestFixture]
public class DetailViewModelTests
{
    // ...

    [Test]
    public async Task Init_ParameterProvided_EntryIsSet()
    {
        // Arrange
```

```
        // Act

        // Assert
    }
}
```

2. Next, update the Arrange portion of the test method by creating a new mocked instance of a `TripLogEntry` object to pass to the `Init` method in order to test its functionality. Also, set the ViewModel's `Entry` property to `null` so we can easily confirm that the property has a proper value after calling `Init` later in the Assert portion of the test.

```
[Test]
public async Task Init_ParameterProvided_EntryIsSet()
{
    // Arrange
    var mockEntry = new Mock<TripLogEntry> ().Object;
    _vm.Entry = null;

    // Act

    // Assert
}
```

3. Next, pass the mocked `TripLogEntry` object into the ViewModel's `Init` method in the Act portion of the test method:

```
[Test]
public async Task Init_ParameterProvided_EntryIsSet()
{
    // Arrange
    var mockEntry = new Mock<TripLogEntry> ().Object;
    _vm.Entry = null;

    // Act
    await _vm.Init (mockEntry);
    // Assert
}
```

4. Finally, check that the ViewModel's Entry property is no longer `null` using the NUnit `Assert.IsNotNull` method:

```
[Test]
public async Task Init_ParameterProvided_EntryIsSet()
{
```

```
// Arrange
var mockEntry = new Mock<TripLogEntry> ().Object;
_vm.Entry = null;

// Act
await _vm.Init (mockEntry);

// Assert
Assert.IsNotNull (_vm.Entry, "Entry is null after being
initialized with a valid TripLogEntry object.");
}
```

 There are several other Assert methods such as
AreEqual, IsTrue, and IsFalse that can be
used for various types of assertions.

Notice the second parameter in the Assert.IsNotNull method, which is an optional parameter. This allows you to provide a message to be displayed if the test fails to help troubleshoot the code under the test.

We should include a test to ensure the ViewModel throws an exception if the empty Init method is called, because the DetailViewModel requires the use of the Init method in the base class that takes a parameter. We can do this using the Assert. Throws NUnit method and providing a delegate that calls the Init method:

```
[Test]
public void Init_ParameterNotProvided_
ThrowsEntryNotProvidedException()
{
    // Assert
    Assert.Throws (typeof (EntryNotProvidedException), async () =>
    {
        await _vm.Init ();
    });
}
```

Initially, this test will fail because until this point, we have not included the code to throw an EntryNotProvidedException in DetailViewModel. In fact, the tests currently will not even build because we have not defined the EntryNotProvidedException type.

In order to get the tests to build, create a new class in the core library that inherits from `Exception` and name it `EntryNotProvidedException`:

```
public class EntryNotProvidedException : Exception
{
    public EntryNotProvidedException () : base ("An Entry object
was not provided. If using DetailViewModel, be sure to use the Init
overload that takes an Entry parameter.")
    {
    }
}
```

Now, if we run the tests, the first one will pass; and the second test, the one that asserts that calls to an empty `Init` method throws an exception, will fail. In order to get this test to pass, we just need to override the empty `Init` method in `DetailViewModel` and have it throw `EntryNotProvidedException`:

```
public class DetailViewModel : BaseViewModel<TripLogEntry>
{
    // ...

    public override async Task Init ()
    {
        throw new EntryNotProvidedException ();
    }

    public override async Task Init (TripLogEntry logEntry)
    {
        Entry = logEntry;
    }
}
```

For ViewModels that have dependencies on specific functionality of a service, you will need to provide an additional setup when you mock the objects for its constructor. For example, the `NewEntryViewModel` depends on the `GetGeoCoordinatesAsync` method of `ILocationService` in order to get the user's current location in the `Init` method. By simply providing a new `Mock` object for `ILocationService` to ViewModel, this method will return null and an exception will be thrown when setting the `Latitude` and `Longitude` properties.

In order to overcome this, we just need to use the Setup method when creating Mock to define how the calls to the GetGeoCoordinatesAsync method should be returned to the callers of the mock ILocationService instance:

1. Create a new class in the TripLog.Tests project named NewEntryViewModelTests. Add the TextFixture attribute to the class, just as we did with the DetailViewModelTests class:

```
[TestFixture]
public class NewEntryViewModelTests
{ }
```

2. Next, create a Setup method with the [Setup] attribute where we will define the NewEntryViewModel instance that will be used by tests in the class. NewEntryViewModel requires four parameters. We will use Moq again to provide mock implementations for them, but we need to customize the implementation for ILocationService to specify exactly what the GetGeoCoordinatesAsync method should return. By doing this, we can properly assert all the values in the ViewModel that come from the GetGetoCoordinatesAsync method:

```
[TestFixture]
public class NewEntryViewModelTests
{
    NewEntryViewModel _vm;

    [SetUp]
    public void Setup()
    {
        var locMock = new Mock<ILocationService> ();
        locMock
            .Setup (x => x.GetGeoCoordinatesAsync ())
            .ReturnsAsync (
                new GeoCoords {
                    Latitude = 123,
                    Longitude = 321
                }
        );

        _vm = new NewEntryViewModel (
            new Mock<INavService> ().Object,
            locMock.Object,
            new Mock<ITripLogDataService> ().Object);
    }
}
```

Now that we know our mock ILocationService implementation will return
123 for latitude and 321 for longitude, we can properly test the ViewModel's Init
method and ensure that the Latitude and Longitude properties are properly set
by using its provided ILocationService (this would be an actual platform-specific
implementation when running the mobile app).

Following the Arrange-Act-Assert pattern, set the values of the Latitude and
Longitude properties to 0 before calling the Init method. In the Assert portion of
the test, confirm that after calling Init, the Latitude and Longitude properties
of ViewModel are the values that we expect to come from the provided mock
ILocationService instance—123 and 321:

```
[TestFixture]
public class NewEntryViewModelTests
{
    // ...

    [Test]
    public async Task Init_EntryIsSetWithGeoCoordinates()
    {
        // Arrange
        _vm.Latitude = 0.0;
        _vm.Longitude = 0.0;

        // Act
        await _vm.Init ();

        // Assert
        Assert.AreEqual (123, _vm.Latitude);
        Assert.AreEqual (321, _vm.Longitude);
    }
}
```

It is important to recognize that we are not testing the actual result of the
ILocationService method—we are testing that the Init method that calls the
ILocationService method will properly run and process the results of that method.
The best way to do this is with mock objects—especially for platform-specific services
or services that provide dynamic or inconsistent data.

As you can see, the use of dependency injection in the app architecture makes it
extremely easy to test our ViewModels with maximum flexibility and minimum code.

Running unit tests in Xamarin Studio

Once you have some unit tests created, you can start running them directly from Xamarin Studio. Typically, this should be done as tests are created throughout your development lifecycle as well as before you commit your code to source control, especially if there is a build pipeline that will automatically run the tests.

To run the unit tests that we just created, navigate to **Run | Run Unit Tests** with the `TripLog.Tests` project selected in the **Solution** pane; otherwise, right-click on the `TripLog.Tests` project in the **Solution** pane and click on **Run**. After the tests have completed running, the results will appear in the **Test Results** pane:

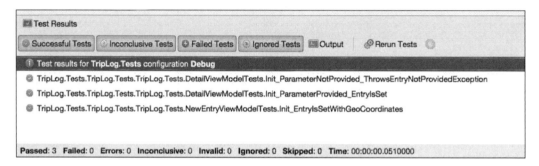

If the test fails, you will see the failure along with the **Stack Trace** in the **Test Results** pane:

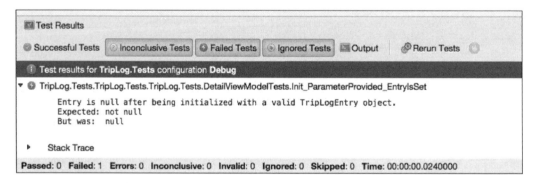

Notice the message that we provided in the `Assert.IsNotNull` method is shown in the failure result.

Automated UI testing

While unit tests ensure that a significant amount of code is tested, it is specifically focused on testing the logic within the app, leaving the user interface largely untested. This is where UI testing comes into play. UI testing allows us to automate specific actions within the app's user interface to assert that they function properly—just like regular unit tests assert that business logic delivers the desired results or functionality.

Xamarin provides a very rich set of tools for performing automated UI tests—both locally and in the Xamarin Test Cloud. UI tests can be written in C# and NUnit using Xamarin's UITest framework or in Ruby using Xamarin's Calabash framework. For the purposes of this book, we will only focus on using the C# approach using Xamarin.UITest.

The Xamarin UITest framework

The UITest framework enables you to automate interactions with an app using C# and the NUnit testing suite. All interactions take place through an instance of IApp. The ConfigureApp class is used to create iOS and Android IApp instances. We will take a closer look at creating IApp instances with ConfigureApp in the next couple of sections.

At the time of writing this book, UITest only supports iOS and Android.

Common UITest methods

The UITest framework contains many APIs that can be used for interacting with an app's user interface. Here are some of the more commonly used methods and the ones we will specifically use to test the TripLog app in this chapter.

These methods are members of the IApp interface:

- Screenshot(): This is used to take a screenshot of the current state of the app
- Tap(): This is used to send a tap interaction to a specific element on the app's current screen
- EnterText() and ClearText(): These are used to add and remove text from input elements such as Entry views in Xamarin.Forms
- Query(): This is used to find elements on the app's current screen
- Repl: This is used to interact in real-time with the app through the terminal using the UITest API
- WaitForElement(): This is used to hold up the test until a specific element appears on the app's current screen within a specific timeout period

Many of the previous methods, including `Query` and `WaitForElement`, return an `AppResult[]` object that can be used to determine the results of the call. For example, if a `Query` call returns an empty result set, then we can assert that the element does not exist. We will see a couple uses of this in the next section when we start writing actual tests.

These methods are members of the `AppQuery` class and are typically used in the `AppQuery Func` parameters of the `IApp` methods mentioned previously:

- `Class()`: This is used to find elements on the app's current screen based on their class type
- `Marked()`: This is used to find elements on the app's current screen based on their text or identifier
- `Css()`: This is used to perform CSS selector operations on the contents of a webview on the app's current screen

Creating a UITest project in Xamarin Studio

Our UI tests will run side-by-side the normal unit tests in our solution:

Create a new Xamarin UITest project within the `Tests` solution folder and name it `TripLog.UITests`:

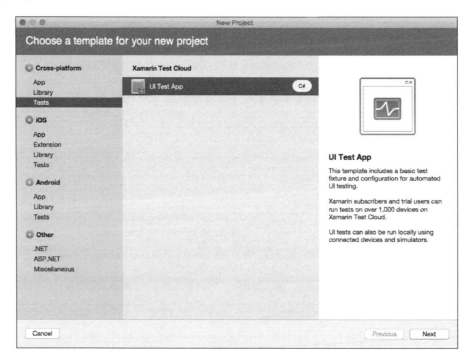

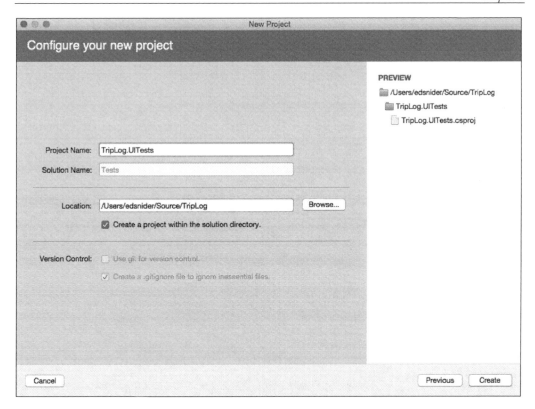

By default, we are supplied with an initial file named `Tests.cs`. We will place our UI tests in this single `Tests.cs` file for now. In some cases, it might make sense to break your UI tests up into separate files. In addition to the `Tests.cs` class, we are also provided with a class named `AppInitializer.cs`, which is used by the `Tests.cs` class to create an `IApp` instance and start the app under the test.

Initializing the TripLog app for UITest

In order to start an app and interact with it via UITest, we must perform some initialization steps, which occur in the `AppInitializer` class. The `AppInitializer` class has a static method called `StartApp`, which is called by the Tests setup method to get an `IApp` instance. It can be either an `iOSApp` or an `AndroidApp` using the `ConfigureApp` class:

```
public class AppInitializer
{
    public static IApp StartApp (Platform platform)
    {
```

```
        if (platform == Platform.Android) {
            return ConfigureApp
                .Android
                // TODO: Update this path ...
                //.ApkFile ("../../../Droid/bin/Debug/TripLog.apk")
                .StartApp ();
        }

        return ConfigureApp
            .iOS
            // TODO: Update this path ...
            //.AppBundle ("../../../iOS/bin/iPhoneSimulator/Debug/
    TripLog.iOS.app")
            .StartApp ();
    }
}
```

Notice that the `ApkFile` and `AppBundle` methods are currently commented out. This is because it is not required to run the tests locally within the unit test pane in Xamarin Studio.

Testing views

We will create tests for specific scenarios within the app to assert that screens and elements within them appear when expected and to capture screenshots of each step of each scenario for visual inspection.

When testing the UI, we will use a combination of the Xamarin.UITest and NUnit frameworks. UITest allows us to query and interact with elements on the app's user interface, whereas NUnit allows us to apply assertions to the results of the UITest operations resulting in either a pass or fail of the test—similar to typical unit tests.

The first scenario to test in our TripLog app is signing in. The main steps in our sign in scenario are as follows:

- Tap the **Sign in with Facebook** button on the first screen
- The OAuth webview authentication screen appears with the Facebook sign in form
- Enter valid Facebook credentials and tap on the **log in** button within the webview
- The main screen of the app containing the TripLog entries list appears

In order to create a UI test for the sign in scenario, perform the following steps:

1. First, create a new method in the `Tests` file named `SignIn` and decorate it with the `[Test]` attribute:

```
[Test]
public void SignIn ()
{ }
```

2. Add a private method named `PerformFacebookSignInSteps` to the `Tests` class that will handle the test steps specific to the Facebook sign in process. By placing these test steps into a separate method, they are easily reused in other tests that will also require automating the login process before carrying out other steps within the UI:

```
void PerformFacebookSignInSteps (string email,
    string password)
{
    // Wait for sign in with Facebook button to appear
    app.WaitForElement (x => x.Text ("Sign in with Facebook"));

    app.Tap (x => x.Text ("Sign in with Facebook"));

    // Wait for Login button within Facebook oAuth webview to
appear
    app.WaitForElement (x => x.WebView().Css ("[name=login]"));

    app.Screenshot ("Facebook oAuth login screen");

    // Enter text in the element within the webview with
name="email"
    app.EnterText (x => x.WebView ().Css ("[name=email]"), email);

    // Enter text in the element within the webview with
name="email"
    app.EnterText (x => x.WebView ().Css ("[name=pass]"),
password);

    // Tap the button in the webview with name="login"
    app.Tap (x => x.WebView ().Css ("[name=login]"));
}
```

3. Next, update the `SignIn` test method to call the `PerformFacebookSignInSteps` method, and validate that the main screen appears after successfully signing in:

```
[Test]
public void SignIn ()
{
    app.Screenshot ("Sign in screen");

    PerformFacebookSignInSteps ("<your-fb-email>", "<your-fb-
password>");

    var mainScreen = app.WaitForElement (x => x.Marked
("TripLog").Class ("UINavigationBar"));

    app.Screenshot ("Main screen");

    // Assert main screen is shown
    Assert.IsTrue (mainScreen.Any (), "Main screen wasn't shown
after signing in");
}
```

We can also write UI tests for alternative scenarios such as when the user taps the **Cancel** button on the OAuth web view authentication screen:

```
[Test]
public void CancelSignIn ()
{
    app.Screenshot ("Sign in screen");

    app.Tap (x => x.Text ("Sign in with Facebook"));

    // Wait for Login button within Facebook oAuth webview to appear
    app.WaitForElement (x => x.WebView().Css ("[name=login]"));

    // According to REPL there are 3 elements marked as Cancel - the
one at the second 2nd index is a UIButtonLabel which we need
    var cancel = app.Query (x => x.Marked ("Cancel").Index (2));

    // Assert there is a Cancel button the UINavigationBar
    Assert.IsTrue (cancel.Any ());

    app.Screenshot ("Authentication screen with Cancel button");

    app.Tap (x => x.Marked ("Cancel").Index (2));
```

```
    // Wait for sign in screen to appear
    var mainScreen = app.WaitForElement (x => x.Marked ("Sign in with
Facebook"));

    // Assert sign in screen is shown after auth webview screen is
canceled
    Assert.IsTrue (mainScreen.Any ());

    app.Screenshot ("Sign in screen after auth is canceled");
}
```

The second scenario that we can test is adding a new entry. The main steps in this scenario are as follows:

- Tap the **Sign in with Facebook** button on the first screen
- The OAuth webview authentication screen appears with the Facebook sign in form
- Enter valid Facebook credentials and tap on the **log in** button within the webview
- The main screen of the app containing the TripLog entries list appears
- Tap the **New** button on the main screen
- The new entry screen appears
- Fill out the form on the new entry screen
- Tap the **Save** button on the new entry screen
- The main screen of the app containing the TripLog entries list appears

We will need to use the `PerformFacebookSignInSteps` method again to advance through the sign in steps:

```
[Test]
public void AddNewEntry ()
{
    app.Screenshot ("Sign in screen");

    PerformFacebookSignInSteps ("<your-fb-email>", "<your-fb-
password>");

    // Wait for main screen to appear
    var mainScreen = app.WaitForElement (x => x.Marked ("TripLog").
Class ("UINavigationBar"));

    app.Screenshot ("Main screen");
```

```
    // Assert main screen is shown
    Assert.IsTrue (mainScreen.Any (), "Main screen wasn't shown after
signing in");

    app.Tap (x => x.Marked ("New"));

    // Wait for New Entry screen to appear
    var newEntryScreen = app.WaitForElement (x => x.Marked ("New
Entry").Class ("UINavigationBar"));

    app.Screenshot ("New entry screen");

    // Assert New Entry screen is shown
    Assert.IsTrue (newEntryScreen.Any (), "New Entry screen was not
shown after tapping New on main screen");

    // Enter title text into Title EntryCell (first EntryCell)
    app.EnterText (x => x.Class ("Xamarin_Forms_Platform_iOS_
EntryCellRenderer_EntryCellTableViewCell").Index (0),
        "Test Entry");

    // Tap into Date EntryCell (fourth EntryCell)
    app.Tap (x => x.Class ("Xamarin_Forms_Platform_iOS_
EntryCellRenderer_EntryCellTableViewCell").Index (3));

    // Tap Done on the date picker
    app.Tap (x => x.Marked ("Done"));

    // Tap into Rating EntryCell (fifth EntryCell) and assert numeric
keyboard
    app.Tap (x => x.Class ("Xamarin_Forms_Platform_iOS_
EntryCellRenderer_EntryCellTableViewCell").Index (4));

    var numericKeyboard = app.Query (x => x.Class("UIKBKeyView"));

    // Assert numeric keyboard is shown for Rating EntryCell - numeric
keyboard has 12 UIKBKeyViews
    Assert.IsTrue (numericKeyboard.Count () == 12, "Rating EntryCell
doesn't use numeric keyboard");

    // Clear default text in Rating EntryCell (fourth EntryCell)
    app.ClearText (x => x.Class ("Xamarin_Forms_Platform_iOS_
EntryCellRenderer_EntryCellTableViewCell")
```

```
                          .Index (4)
                          .Descendant ("UITextField"));


      // Enter rating text into Rating EntryCell (fifth EntryCell)
      app.EnterText (x => x.Class ("Xamarin_Forms_Platform_iOS_
EntryCellRenderer_EntryCellTableViewCell")
                          .Index (4)
                          .Descendant ("UITextField"),
          "3");


      // Enter notes text into Notes EntryCell (sixth EntryCell)
      app.EnterText (x => x.Class ("Xamarin_Forms_Platform_iOS_
EntryCellRenderer_EntryCellTableViewCell")
          .Index (5)
          .Descendant ("UITextField"),
          "Test entry notes.");


      // Tap Save to exit the new entry screen
      app.Tap (x => x.Marked ("Save"));


      // Wait for main screen to appear
      mainScreen = app.WaitForElement (x => x.Marked ("TripLog").Class
("UINavigationBar"));


      // Assert main screen is shown after saving a new entry
      Assert.IsTrue (mainScreen.Any (), "Main screen was not shown after
saving a new entry");
      }
```

Notice that a common pattern used to validate screens and elements is to use the
`WaitForElement` method in the UITest API along with the NUnit `Assert.IsTrue`
method.

> There are a few references to iOS specifics throughout
> these tests. Use the private platform class variable to
> check the platform and handle accordingly for Android.
> Alternatively, if these tests will only be run for iOS, then
> remove the `[TestFixture (Platform.Android)]`
> class attribute; the tests will be locked to iOS only.

Running UI tests

In order to run UI tests, **Xamarin Test Cloud Agent** needs to be included in the app project. For Android, Test Cloud Agent is provided by the UITest framework, and so, it does not need to be manually added. For iOS, Test Cloud Agent needs to be manually added to the project either via NuGet or Xamarin component:

1. Add a reference to the Xamarin.TestCloud.Agent NuGet package to the TripLog.iOS project.

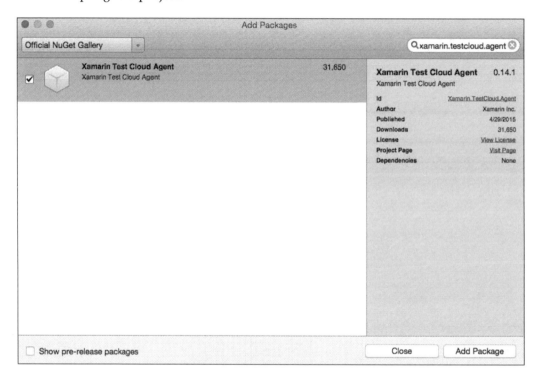

2. Update the `FinishedLaunching` method of the TripLog app `AppDelegate` class to start Test Cloud Agent. Again, this step is only for iOS app projects:

```
public override bool FinishedLaunching (UIApplication app,
NSDictionary options)
{
    global::Xamarin.Forms.Forms.Init ();

    Xamarin.FormsMaps.Init ();

    #if ENABLE_TEST_CLOUD
    Xamarin.Calabash.Start ();
```

```
#endif

LoadApplication (new App (new TripLogPlatformModule()));

return base.FinishedLaunching (app, options);
}
```

Notice the use of the ENABLE_TEST_CLOUD compiler symbol in the #if directive surrounding the Calabash.Start method call. This ensures that Test Cloud Agent is only started under specific configurations. Be sure to include the ENABLE_TEST_CLOUD symbol in the **Debug** configuration only and not in the **Release** configuration.

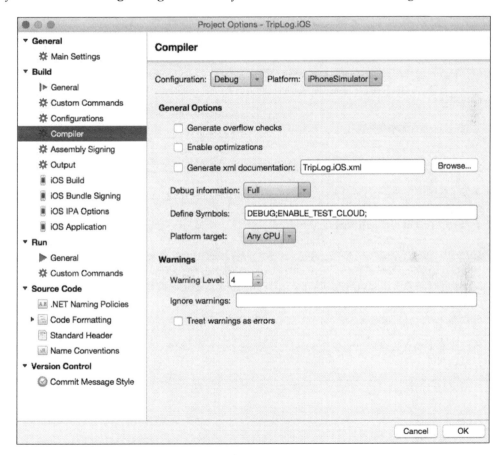

 In most cases, when creating a new iOS project, the Test Cloud Agent NuGet package will already be added to the project references and the Calabash.Start method call will already be included in the AppDelegate.

Running UI tests locally

UI tests can be run from the **Unit Tests** pane within Xamarin Studio, just like normal unit tests. However, you will notice that there is a **Test Apps** node within the **TripLog.UITests** section.

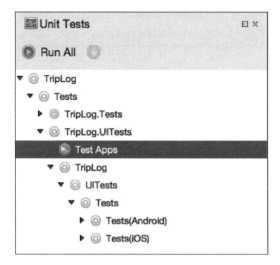

You need to either add your app to the **Test Apps** node of the **Unit Tests** pane or specify the path to the app in the `AppInitializer` class mentioned earlier; otherwise, your tests will fail to run.

To add your apps to the **Tests Apps** node within the **Unit Tests** pane, simply right-click on the **Test Apps** item and click on **Add App Project**. This will bring up a dialog that allows you to select one or many UITest compatible projects that can be added.

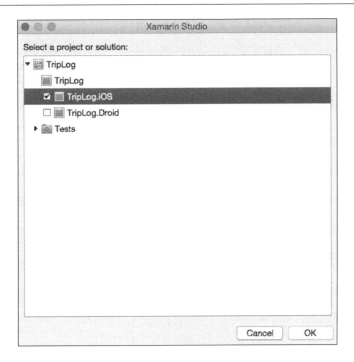

Select the project(s) that you want to add to the tests and click on **OK**. For the purpose of this chapter, we only need to select the TripLog.iOS app project since our tests are specific to iOS. You will now see the selected app listed under the **Test Apps** node in the **Unit Tests** pane.

If you don't see your iOS app project listed in the dialog when trying to add to the **Test Apps** node, ensure that you have added the Xamarin Test Cloud Agent NuGet package to your iOS project.

Once you have either added your app projects to the **Unit Tests** or referenced the app package within `AppInitializer`, simply run the UI tests within the **Unit Tests** pane, just as you do for normal unit tests.

When your UI tests start to run, the UITest framework will automatically deploy your app to the simulator, run the app, and step through each of the steps specified in the test methods. The results of the tests will appear in the **Test Results** pane in Xamarin Studio.

Enabling screenshots

By default, screenshots are not stored when UI tests are run locally. In order to store the screenshots captured during your tests, you must add the `EnableLocalScreenshots` method to the `ConfigureApp` method chain in the `AppInitializer` class:

```
return ConfigureApp
    .iOS
    .EnableLocalScreenshots ()
    .StartApp ();
```

Once enabled, the screenshot images will be stored in the `bin` output folder where the tests are run from. Beware that these images will be overwritten the next time the tests run. So, copy them out to a different location if they need to be stored for each local test run.

Running UI tests in Xamarin Test Cloud

Once you have run your UI tests locally and verified the steps within them, you can broaden the number of devices, screen sizes, and operating system versions that they run on by uploading them to Xamarin Test Cloud.

You can upload your UI tests to Xamarin Test Cloud directly from the **Unit Tests** pane in Xamarin Studio.

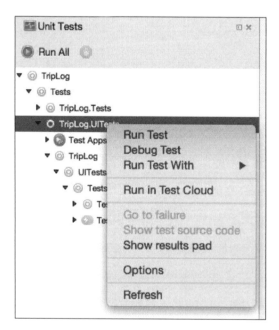

Xamarin Studio will build and upload your app and UI tests to Test Cloud. Once it has finished uploading the app and tests to Test Cloud, it will automatically launch the Test Cloud interface in your browser and allow you to select the parameters for the test run including specific devices and operating system versions. Finally, it will validate the tests and run them on the selected devices, providing the test results at completion.

Summary

In this chapter, we looked into how to take advantage of the loosely coupled architecture that we have developed in the earlier chapters of this book to write unit tests. We used a mocking framework to mock out the services that our ViewModels are dependent on to be able to effectively test the logic within them. We also looked at how to leverage Xamarin's UITest framework to write and run UI tests both locally and in Xamarin's Test Cloud environment.

9
App Analytics

In this last chapter of the book, we are going to focus on application analytics and crash reporting, and how they can help ensure the ongoing quality of an app. Specifically, we will look at the **Xamarin Insights** toolset, and how to integrate it into the TripLog Xamarin.Forms mobile app that we have created throughout the book.

Here is a quick look at what we'll cover in this chapter:

- Mobile app analytics and crash reporting
- Adding Xamarin Insights to the TripLog app

Mobile app analytics and crash reporting

Application analytic and crash reporting tools have been around for a long time. The idea of application analytics is to collect data about your users, their behavior within your application, the features they use (or don't use), and how often they use the application or specific features of the application. The idea of crash reporting is to collect crash or error data from within the application. In both cases, the information collected is typically aggregated into a single dashboard-like interface so that you and other developers on the application team can analyze it.

Application analytics are also extremely important to a product's lifecycle and stakeholders, as it provides real insight into the application and can help drive key business decisions around the product. For example, a feature that was thought to be very important to users might show up in analytics data as something users are not actually using as much as anticipated. From there, the decision needs to be made whether this is because the feature is undiscoverable or simply not as important to the users as anticipated. On the other hand, analytics might indicate that a specific feature or area within your application is being used or accessed far more than expected. This would tell the product owners and developers that focusing on that feature or area should be a priority.

The power of a crash reporting tool is that it automatically captures the exception and stack trace information. Without this type of capability, you as a developer are left to rely on your end user to report the bug or error. In some cases, they may not even report the error and will simply close your app, and you will have no idea to even address the bug. Assuming your users do report back to you about a bug or error they witnessed in the application, you are still relying on them to provide you with accurate information and are left trying to reproduce the error. Not only is this a potentially inaccurate process but it is also time consuming and cumbersome. It puts a burden on your users, as well as you and your development team. Having a crash reporting tool in place allows you to handle bugs and errors in real-time, which is much faster than relying on users. If a user does experience a bug and reports it to you, having the crash reporting tool integrated within your app allows you to easily find the data related to the error they ran into. Furthermore, if you have both app analytics and crash reporting in your application, you can often leverage the analytics to identify the specific path the user took within the application before running into the issue.

There are several tools on the market, some that only do analytics, others that only do crash reporting, and, of course, some that do both. Most of the tools support .NET, and several specifically support Xamarin, making it easy to integrate them into mobile applications built with Xamarin.

Xamarin Insights

Xamarin Insights is a product offered by Xamarin that provides both analytics and crash reporting in a single toolset. It is by far one of the best and most feature-rich tools on the market, and because it's made by Xamarin, it's very easy to use with apps built on the Xamarin platform. For the purposes of this book, we will leverage the Xamarin Insights tool to add analytics and crash reporting capabilities to our TripLog app. However, due to the loosely coupled nature we have implemented in our app, the concepts used in this chapter to use Xamarin Insights could be used for pretty much any other analytic or crash reporting tool that supports .NET.

Setting up Xamarin Insights

Using Xamarin Insights in your mobile app is pretty straightforward. You just need to include the `Xamarin.Insights` NuGet package in each of your projects and set your app up in the Xamarin Insights web-based dashboard at `http://insights.xamarin.com/`. When you set your app up, you will be given an API key that you need to include in your code when you initialize the Insights library. Fortunately, if you're using Xamarin Studio, Xamarin has made all of this extremely easy by building it right into the options dialog for iOS and Android projects.

In order to set up Xamarin Insights, perform the following steps:

1. Open the **Project Options** dialog by either double clicking or right clicking the **TripLog.iOS** project.

2. Select the **Insights** item on the left side of the **Project Options** dialog:

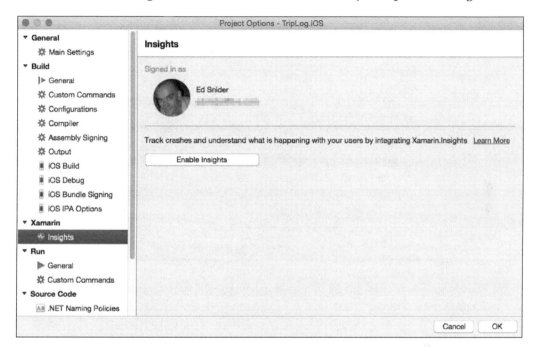

3. Click the **Enable Insights** button.

4. Repeat steps 1 through 3 for the `TripLog.Droid` project.

5. Add the `Xamarin.Insights` NuGet package to the TripLog core project.

With Xamarin Insights all set up and configured for each platform project, we can start using it immediately to send crash reports and usage data. However, just like the other platform specific capabilities we implemented earlier in the book, we want to decouple the analytics implementation from the rest of the app. In the next section, we will create an analytics service that can be used in our app through dependency, keeping the architecture flexible and easy to test.

Creating an analytics service

In order to use Xamarin Insights in our TripLog app, we will want to abstract it into a service, like we did for geo-location. As we have seen multiple times in previous chapters, there are numerous benefits to this approach, namely, it loosely couples our ViewModels from the actual code that uses the Xamarin Insights API, making unit testing our ViewModels much simpler and cleaner.

In order to create an analytics service, perform the following steps:

1. First, create a new interface named `IAnalyticsService` in the `Services` folder in core library:

   ```
   public interface IAnalyticsService
   { }
   ```

2. Next, update the `IAnalyticsService` interface with methods to send crash reports and track usage events:

   ```
   public interface IAnalyticsService
   {
       void SendCrashReport(Exception exception);
       void SendCrashReport(Exception exception, IDictionary<string,
   string> additionalData);
       void TrackEvent(string @event);
       void TrackEvent(string @event, IDictionary<string, string>
   additionalData);
       void RegisterUser(string userId, IDictionary<string, string>
   additionalData);
   }
   ```

Notice that the methods in this service are not necessarily specific to Xamarin Insights—they represent pretty generic functionality when it comes to error and event tracking. This leads to yet another benefit of the loosely coupled architecture that we have put in place: if, for some reason, you needed to stop using Xamarin Insights and use another app analytics toolset instead, you would simply write a new implementation of this interface, and your ViewModels will automatically be ready to use the new implementation, since they use it through the `IAnalyticsService` interface.

For now, we will of course use Xamarin Insights in the concrete implementation of the `IAnalyticsService` interface. The Xamarin Insights API is pretty simple and straightforward, and so the implementation for each of the methods in the interface is no more than a couple of lines. Specifically, the `Xamarin.Insights.Report` method allows us to send `Exception` data to the Xamarin Insights dashboard, and the `Xamarin.Insights.Track` method allows us to send user events to the dashboard.

The purpose of this chapter is to show how an analytics library can be integrated into a Xamarin.Forms mobile app using the patterns implemented in this book. For more information about the Xamarin Insights toolset and the capabilities of its SDK, checkout the documentation at `http://insights.xamarin.com/`.

In order to create the Xamarin Insights implementation of `IAnalyticsService`, perform the following steps:

1. Create a new class named `XamarinInsightsAnalyticsService` in the `Services` folder in the core library that implements `IAnalyticsService`:

```
public class XamarinInsightsAnalyticsService
    : IAnalyticsService
{ }
```

2. Next, implement the members of `IAnalyticsService` within the `XamarinInsightsAnalyticsService`:

```
public class XamarinInsightsAnalyticsService
: IAnalyticsService
{
    #region IAnalyticsService implementation

    public void SendCrashReport(Exception exception)
    {
        Insights.Report(exception, Insights.Severity.Error);
    }

    public void SendCrashReport(Exception exception,
IDictionary<string, string> additionalData)
    {
        Insights.Report(exception, new Dictionary<string,
string>(additionalData), Insights.Severity.Error);
    }

    public void TrackEvent(string @event)
    {
        Insights.Track(@event);
    }

    public void TrackEvent(string @event, IDictionary<string,
string> additionalData)
    {
```

```
            Insights.Track(@event, additionalData);
        }

        public void RegisterUser(string userId, IDictionary<string,
    string> additionalData)
        {
            Insights.Identify(userId, additionalData);
        }

        #endregion
    }
```

3. Next, update the `TripLogCoreModule` in the core library to register the `XamarinInsightsAnalyticsService` implementation into the IoC:

```
public class TripLogCoreModule : NinjectModule
{
    public override void Load ()
    {
        // ViewModels
        // ...

        // Core Services
        // ...

        Bind<IAnalyticsService> ()
          .To<XamarinInsightsAnalyticsService> ()
          .InSingletonScope ();
    }
}
```

Next, we need to be able to use this new analytics service within the logic of our app, specifically the ViewModels. Because we will likely need to report analytic data from all of our ViewModels, it would be best to just include an instance of `IAnalyticsService` as a property of the `BaseViewModel`, similar to the `INavService` property, and include it in the constructor's parameter list:

```
public abstract class BaseViewModel : INotifyPropertyChanged
{
    protected INavService NavService { get; private set; }
    protected IAnalyticsService AnalyticsService { get; private set; }

    // ...

    protected BaseViewModel (INavService navService,
```

```
       IAnalyticsService analyticsService)
    {
       NavService = navService;
       AnalyticsService = analyticsService;
    }

    // ...
}
```

We also need to update the constructor of the `BaseViewModel<TParameter>` class
that subclasses the `BaseViewModel` class to take an `IAnalyticsService` parameter,
which it simply passes to its base class:

```
public abstract class BaseViewModel<TParameter> : BaseViewModel
{
    protected BaseViewModel (INavService navService,
        IAnalyticsService analyticsService)
        : base (navService, analyticsService)
    { }

    // ...
}
```

Finally, we need to update the constructors of each of the ViewModels that inherit
from `BaseViewModel` to take an `IAnalyticsService` parameter, which is just passed
to its `BaseViewModel` base class.

Tracking exceptions and events

Now that we have an `IAnalyticsService` property in all of our ViewModels,
we can update all of our `try/catch` blocks to pass exceptions to Xamarin Insights.
For example, in `MainViewModel`, we have a `try/finally` block in the `LoadEntries`
method that is currently not catching exceptions.

Update this `try` block with a `catch` block and then pass the caught `Exception` off to
the analytics service via the `SendCrashReport` method:

```
void LoadEntries()
{
    if (IsBusy)
        return;

    IsBusy = true;

    try
    {
        // ...
```

```
    }
    catch (Exception e) {
        AnalyticsService.SendCrashReport (e);
    }
    finally {
        IsBusy = false;
    }
}
```

 Xamarin Insights automatically reports all unhandled exceptions (exceptions that are not handled in a `try`/`catch` block) once it has been initialized in the app.

We can also start tracking user events throughout the application. For example, if we wanted to know how often users went to the New Entry page in our app, we could call the `TrackEvent` method of our `IAnalyticsService` within the `Init` method of `NewEntryViewModel` to log that in Xamarin Insights:

```
public class NewEntryViewModel : BaseViewModel
{
    // ...

    public NewEntryViewModel (INavService navService, ILocationService
    locService, IPhotoService photoService, ITripLogDataService
    tripLogService, IAnalyticsService analyticsService)
        : base (navService, analyticsService)
    {
        // ...
    }

    public override async Task Init ()
    {
        AnalyticsService.TrackEvent ("New Entry Page");

        // ...
    }

    // ...
}
```

Summary

In this chapter, we covered the importance of crash reporting and event tracking capabilities in mobile applications. We built an analytics service that abstracts away a Xamarin Insights implementation and that can be used to handle both capabilities within our ViewModels.

Index

Thank you for buying
Mastering Xamarin.Forms

About Packt Publishing

Packt, pronounced 'packed', published its first book, *Mastering phpMyAdmin for Effective MySQL Management*, in April 2004, and subsequently continued to specialize in publishing highly focused books on specific technologies and solutions.

Our books and publications share the experiences of your fellow IT professionals in adapting and customizing today's systems, applications, and frameworks. Our solution-based books give you the knowledge and power to customize the software and technologies you're using to get the job done. Packt books are more specific and less general than the IT books you have seen in the past. Our unique business model allows us to bring you more focused information, giving you more of what you need to know, and less of what you don't.

Packt is a modern yet unique publishing company that focuses on producing quality, cutting-edge books for communities of developers, administrators, and newbies alike. For more information, please visit our website at www.packtpub.com.

About Packt Open Source

In 2010, Packt launched two new brands, Packt Open Source and Packt Enterprise, in order to continue its focus on specialization. This book is part of the Packt Open Source brand, home to books published on software built around open source licenses, and offering information to anybody from advanced developers to budding web designers. The Open Source brand also runs Packt's Open Source Royalty Scheme, by which Packt gives a royalty to each open source project about whose software a book is sold.

Writing for Packt

We welcome all inquiries from people who are interested in authoring. Book proposals should be sent to author@packtpub.com. If your book idea is still at an early stage and you would like to discuss it first before writing a formal book proposal, then please contact us; one of our commissioning editors will get in touch with you.

We're not just looking for published authors; if you have strong technical skills but no writing experience, our experienced editors can help you develop a writing career, or simply get some additional reward for your expertise.

Xamarin Essentials

ISBN: 978-1-78355-083-8   Paperback: 234 pages

Learn how to efficiently develop Android and iOS apps for deployment using the Xamarin platform

1. Explore the Xamarin platform and understand the architecture behind Xamarin.iOS and Xamarin.Android.

2. Learn how to build and run iOS and Android apps using Xamarin Studio and Visual Studio.

3. This is a practical tutorial with a clear and concise approach that teaches you how to create, share, and reuse code across your iOS and Android app.

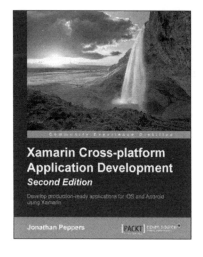

Xamarin Cross-platform Application Development - Second Edition

ISBN: 978-1-78439-788-3   Paperback: 298 pages

Develop production-ready applications for iOS and Android using Xamarin

1. Write native iOS and Android applications with Xamarin.iOS and Xamarin.Android respectively.

2. Learn strategies that allow you to share code between iOS and Android.

3. Design user interfaces that can be shared across Android, iOS, and Windows Phone using Xamarin.Forms.

Please check **www.PacktPub.com** for information on our titles

Xamarin Mobile Application Development for iOS

ISBN: 978-1-78355-918-3   Paperback: 222 pages

If you know C# and have an iOS device, learn to use one language for multiple devices with Xamarin

1. A clear and concise look at how to create your own apps building on what you already know of C#.

2. Create advanced and elegant apps by yourself.

3. Ensure that the majority of your code can also be used with Android and Windows Mobile 8 devices.

Learning Xamarin Studio

ISBN: 978-1-78355-081-4   Paperback: 248 pages

Learn how to build high-performance native applications using the power of Xamarin Studio

1. Get a full introduction to the key features and components of the Xamarin 3 IDE and framework, including Xamarin.Forms and iOS visual designer.

2. Install, integrate and utilise Xamarin Studio with the tools required for building amazing cross-platform applications for iOS and Android.

3. Create, test, and deploy apps for your business and for the app store.

Please check **www.PacktPub.com** for information on our titles

Made in the USA
Columbia, SC
31 January 2018